Notes on

TECHNOLOGY AND THE MORAL ORDER

An advanced study in sociology

———————— *Notes on*

TECHNOLOGY

Alvin W. Gouldner WASHINGTON UNIVERSITY AT ST. LOUIS
and
Richard A. Peterson UNIVERSITY OF WISCONSIN

AND THE MORAL ORDER

With a foreword by Walter R. Goldschmidt
UNIVERSITY OF CALIFORNIA AT LOS ANGELES
And a methodological note by L. Keith Miller
WASHINGTON UNIVERSITY AT ST. LOUIS

THE **BOBBS-MERRILL** COMPANY, INC.
A SUBSIDIARY OF HOWARD W. SAMS & CO., INC.
Publishers • INDIANAPOLIS • NEW YORK

Robert McGinnis
CONSULTING EDITOR
Cornell University

TO THE AUTHORS OF:

The Material Culture and Social Institutions of the Simpler Peoples

L. T. HOBHOUSE
G. C. WHEELER
M. GINSBERG

Preface~~~~

The work reported here was conceived by the authors as part of an ongoing reexamination of functional social theory. As such, it is related to several other studies of functionalism which the senior author has previously published.

In effect, the present study grew out of efforts to find operationalizations for some of these earlier theoretical analyses and, most particularly, to experiment with the use of factor analysis for this purpose. As armchair Xenophons, we found ourselves caught in a theoretical interior from which we sought to improvise a way back to the sea of data. We knew where we wanted to go but were far from certain about the route to be taken or whether there was one. Indeed, our doubts are still far from resolved.

It needs to be said candidly that the data we used were chosen not because of any special interest in them per se, but because they seemed to allow the methodological explorations that *were* of interest. Which is to say that, although we elected to use data deriving from the Human Relations Area Files (that which was then published and easily accessible at the time we undertook our work), nonetheless, we had no expectations of making a contribution to anthropology as such. Should some anthropologists wish to disagree we will not, of course, be churlish. In any event, the original objective was methodological although, as in all such matters, we soon found our interests in substantive issues engaged.

ALVIN W. GOULDNER
RICHARD A. PETERSON

Contents ~~~~

Foreword ∼∼∼∼

Professors Gouldner and Peterson have had the audacity to examine basic philosophic problems with the instruments of modern statistical analysis. These problems are no less than the factors that set the character of human action; the relative importance of the technological aspects of life as against the ethical. If the results are not conclusive, they are titillating; and the promise that such an approach holds should be welcome to all who have endeavored to grapple with social philosophy on the grand level rather than be content to labor in the vineyards.

The audacity is both intellectual and moral. The intellectual boldness lies in facing those areas of moral philosophy in which there already exists a vast, erudite, and inchoate literature. It is an arena where the greatest minds have sought answers, even though these are yet unfound. It is an act of supererogation merely to enter into this field of enquiry.

The audacity is also moral. For the world inhabited by the philosopher and the humanist has always remained alien to that of the scientist. We may be certain—and there are evidences in the wording throughout the essay that the authors themselves are certain—that the very effort will be met by criticism from both sides. For the attitudes of scholars being what they are, there is little doubt that many in each camp will feel that their own approach to discovering the ultimate verities is, in some indefinable way, sullied by the contaminating influence of the other's. The hard-headed scientist will assert that these are soft, undefinable problems; the humanist will assert that violence is done to man's noble conceptions by the very effort to catalog and count—let alone manipulate arithmetically.

Let us examine what the authors have done here. They first review broad theories dealing with the determinants of culture. These they divide fundamentally into two categories. The former are the monolithic theories, such as economic determinism, environmentalism, and the like, which the authors call "single-factor determinism." The second are those theoretical orientations that lose all sense of causality in a cloud of particulars. Among these latter are the currently popular functionalist theories, in which all things interrelate, but none is determinative.

The authors seek a middle ground through the statistical technique of factor analysis. As I understand it, factor analysis is a means of discovering clusters of internally correlated traits which thus tend to form units, presumably reflecting in action some underlying common core of (in this instance) essential human urges. Working with ethnographic data from a sample of the world's societies, they extract several sets of traits by this statistical technique—traits which are highly intercorrelated and which appear to be influential on other aspects of culture.

Of these clusters they treat in detail with four. Two of them have to do with principles of the organization of society: lineality of descent, and male dominance. These they find relatively less important than the other two: the factor that they label "technology," and the factor they label "norm sending," by which they mean ethical orientation or ethos. The drama of their story lies in uncovering the relative importance of these two factors, and to the intellectually curious it is an intensely interesting drama, even though told by the arid methods of statistics.

For, behind the detailed arithmetic and the careful wording, lies what is perhaps the quintessential problem in social science: Is the moral order of a people a result of the techniques by which it gains a livelihood; or is the ethos the determining factor of the character of the total culture? What is particularly significant about this effort is that the authors do not evade the issue. They show that those traits that coalesce as the "norm sending" factor follow closely the Nietzschean definition of Apollonianism. They really are after a statistical answer to this essentially philosophical problem. And they explore their data in a variety of ways to trace out an answer. I must disqualify myself from commenting on these statistical manipulations. All I can say is that first, they have been straightforward in explaining precisely what they have done in as nontechnical a language as possible, and, second, that among my statistically minded sociological friends there will be endless debate over both the legitimacy of these manipulations and the meaning of the results. The authors themselves display a rather engaging uncertainty in this regard, remaining quite aware of the question of the legitimacy of their own acts, and rather more bemused than triumphant over their results. They nowhere shout "Eureka," nor do they close with a Q.E.D. But they do invite you to look at these philosophical questions in the light of statistical procedures.

It would not be giving away too much of their story to discuss the ending here. They found neither of the factors dealing with organization principles, as I have already said, to be very important determinants. They regularly found (by a variety of statistical measures) that both technology and ethos (I find myself embarrassed at the anthropomorphic concept of norm-sending) were the two most influential factors. And between these two there is a consistent, but very slight, balance in favor of the former. They also endeavor to show that the two factors are closely related (with some discussion as to why this is the case) and to examine whether technology is influencing the ethical rather than the other way about. Their results lean toward Steward, White, and Marx, rather than toward Benedict, Malinowski, and Dilthey.

There is comfort in this analysis to those of us who see man's culture as first and foremost an instrumentality for survival—as, broadly speaking, a response to human material needs. There are implications here for evolutionary theory in cultural anthropology, which is inevitably tied in with the notion of the instrumentality of culture. But it is cold comfort for the economic determinists; the data do not support monolithic arguments, but only relative influences.

The significance of the work, however, lies less with the conclusions than with the approach. For it is in the application of modern statistics that we may find our way out of the dilemma between the simple-minded explanations of monolithic theories and the non-explanations that characterize so much anthropological and sociological theory. This is not merely because they are using advanced arithmetic. Statistical treatment of cultural data began with Tylor in his study of "adhesions," and the problem here treated was attacked by Hobhouse, Wheeler, and Ginsberg nearly fifty years ago, by A. L. Kroeber and his associates in the study of culture element distributions, by all those who have worked with data in the Human Relations Area Files, and recently by H. D. Driver and William Massey. Indeed, the last of these, Driver and Massey, endeavored a comparable kind of factorial analysis on American Indian data and addressed the problem of evolution, among other elements. They did this with more factual detail, but less intellectual sophistication. Despite this venerable lineage, Gouldner and Peterson have accomplished something new by bringing the newer statistics to bear and bringing them to bear directly on the problems of social philosophy.

Let us briefly examine what the approach does for two diverse schools of anthropological thought. I am particularly pleased with its implications for Malinowskian functionalism. It may have been useful for Malinowski to assert that all aspects of culture form an interrelated and integrated whole at a time when so much anthropological work was atomistic trait hunting and distributionism. But this functional notion does no more than that; for it offers no explanation as to why culture takes the particular forms it does, nor does it give us any insight into the mechanisms that make it change. (Radcliffe-Brown, it seems to me, was aware of this limitation, but he did not find a way of getting beyond the problem.) Certainly cultures are wholes, but surely we can discover some principles that make them what they are in any particular time and place. What Gouldner and Peterson's approach does is to recognize functional interrelatedness without stopping at that point. It gives a statistical technique for a point I have made before in paraphrasing Orwell:

all things are basic but some are more basic than others. It makes possible a return to causation without giving up the holistic point of view.

On the other hand, the approach is also destructive to so-called "unilinear" evolutionary theory—though, as I have said, not to all evolutionary thought. For unilinear evolution has a monolithic quality which asserts a simple one-to-one relation between mode of production and cultural behavior. The world is more complex than this. The approach here demonstrates this complexity. Kroeber, in his relaxed moments, used to say that taking a stance on theories was like betting on the races; you examine the forms, but in the end you don't know who will win. This study reminds us that, if technology wins by a nose, nevertheless, elements of ethos place close behind, and pay off too. In short, if we are to understand the forces that shape culture, we must look to more than one factor.

The approach offers a middle road between the extremes of single-factor determinism and the attitude that the human scene is either too complex to be understood or is, in fact, not amenable to scientific generalization.

The data in this monograph suggest that technology influences the normative. If it be true for primitive societies, it must also be so for our own. Perhaps it is worth noting that this very study demonstrates the role of technology in such determination. The research here reported would have been all but impossible without modern electronic computer technology. The earlier effort to deal with this problem by Hobhouse, Wheeler, and Ginsberg suffered precisely because it lacked the refinements of modern statistical knowledge and techniques. Thus the existence of modern computer devices has made more feasible the factor analytic approach: that is, to establish clusters of events as meaningful units and thus comprehend the multivalent but not chaotic character of the human scene.

One further comment might be allowed. At this particular moment of our intellectual history, Professor C. P. Snow is making something of a career out of bemoaning the great gulf that lies between the scientist and the humanist. We have already commented on this diversity. Yet, certainly the world that the poet and the mathematicians try to understand is a single world. Certainly they seek to express, each in his own idiom, the truths that characterize the human scene. Neither the complexities of the world itself nor the traditional division of labor in academia can alter or overlook this fact. The complexities may forever be beyond the full understanding of man. Neither the poet nor the physicist, neither the philosopher nor the statistician can unravel all that stands before us. That may well be beyond the combined efforts of all. Yet, it seems to me that a marriage between the intellectual insight of the humanist and the knowledge and techniques of the scientist may bring about a new level of understanding of the nature of our universe. In the realm of human culture, Gouldner and Peterson have made a valiant effort to bring about such a marriage.

WALTER GOLDSCHMIDT
Mbale, Uganda
July 1961

CHAPTER *1*

The Problem 〰️

This exploratory analysis of data from 71 primitive or pre-industrial societies has the following objectives:[1]

1. It seeks to identify fundamental dimensions or subsystems common to such societies, and
2. To examine some of their relations to each other, thus to see them systemically, and
3. To assess the relative importance of these dimensions.
4. It aims to pursue the above objectives with a systematic body of empirical data derived from the Human Relations Area Files and with statistical methods, rather than calling upon random anecdotal materials or impressionistic insight.

The empirical analysis to follow derives from and in turn takes on meaning in terms of certain very general problems. Some of these problems bear on difficulties of theory and research distinctive of the scholarly tradition in anthropology. Others, however, involve meth-

[1] The authors wish to thank the following scholars for their thoughtful criticisms of an earlier draft of this manuscript: John W. Bennett, James Coleman, Robert Hamblin, Irving Kaplan, Walter Goldschmidt, Fred Strodtbeck, and Edward Winter. We are deeply indebted to Kern Dickman of the University of Illinois for help in utilizing Illiac, to the Social Science Research Council for an Auxiliary Research Award which made much of our work possible, and to the Center for Advanced Study in the Behavioral Sciences for typing the manuscript. The authors alone, of course, are responsible for all errors and inadequacies in this study.

odological issues common to both anthropology and sociology alike. It is to the latter, more generic, problems that attention will first be directed.

A Problem of Functional Analysis

The basic methodological outlook of both modern sociology and social anthropology is that of functionalism. Sharing certain precursors in common—notably Durkheim, Radcliffe-Brown, and Malinowski—both these disciplines (if, indeed, they are distinct *scientifically*) are committed to a key postulate, namely: human groups and cultures are to be seen as systems of mutually interdependent elements.

Put in this terse manner, the postulate is almost an item of professional faith, more likely to be given ritualistic reaffirmation than rigorous analytic inspection. To many social scientists the above "system" postulate appears so cogent as to be beyond question. Put in a different yet equivalent form, however, this same postulate is manifestly weak. The weak form of the postulate is this: In social and cultural phenomena, "everything influences everything else."

We take it that there is no operational difference, and hence no difference in substance, between the strong and weak versions of the system postulate. The only difference is in their metaphysical pathos, the former version appearing cogent and somehow significant, while the latter is quite evidently trivial.

The weak form, however, has at least the merit of making it evident that a number of important questions are being begged or ignored. For example, how shall one identify the "everything"—what kind of *operational* measures might be taken to mark out the boundaries of the larger system and to discern the various subsystems of which it may be composed? Just how strongly integrated is this system, or how much "systemness" does it possess? Are the various subsystems equally large or powerful, in terms of their relations to or effects upon one another? To what extent are the component sociocultural elements (or subsystems) part of the same parasystem, and to what extent are they caught up in and do they vary with analytically different domains or parasystems such as the ecological? Is the variance in these different elements equally accountable in terms of the same parasystem? Granted that, by definition, elements in a system are mutually interdependent. Yet one may still ask: are they all interdependent to the same degree, or are some more or less functionally autonomous in relation to a given parasystem or to other subsystems within it? Granted that the elements of a system all influence one another to some degree. Yet one may still ask: do they all influence one another, or the parasystem, to the same extent?

Most of these questions have at least one thing in common: they cannot be answered by qualitative and clinical case studies—indispensable as these are—and they premise for their solution the use of some kind of mathematics. These questions commonly imply that we must begin thinking about and commence making provisional estimates of the varying magnitudes of different system characteristics.

To gain some insight into the manner in which modern social science came to adopt the transparently trivial maxim "everything influences everything else" as a central methodological postulate, it will be useful to take a brief historical excursion. From the standpoint of a broad, bird's-eye perspective, social scientists seem to have used two other basic strategies of analysis prior or alternative to their commitment to functionalism. These are (1) Single Factor Theory and (2) Multiple Causationism.

Single Factor Theory may, for convenience's sake, be taken as the base point in the theoretical development with which we are concerned. In its crudest and "ideal typical" form, this model seemingly asserted that some single factor—e.g., race, climate, or economy—"accounted" for variations in all other cultural and social phenomena, at all times and places. Clearly, however, this is a loose and ambiguous description. Is it possible to state more rigorously the identifying marks of a Single Factor Theory?

Condemned as this model has been by successive generations of social scientists, there should seem to be no difficulty in characterizing it. Yet nothing could be farther from the truth. For example, only rarely did single-factor theories expressly hold that their preferred factor *alone* accounted for *all* social and cultural phenomena. The preferred factor's effect upon others was more likely to be viewed as a "predominant" rather than as an "exclusive" influence. Nor is it at all sure that single-factor theories were invariably characterized by an insistence on the predominance of this single factor at *all* times and places. Witness, for example, the repeated contention in Marxism, often held to be the single-factor theory *par excellence*, that the "forces of production" controlled outcomes only in "the long run," but not at every moment in the social process.

The very term "single factor" is in itself unclear. What, for example, would *not* be a "single factor"? If this question is considered on a purely conceptual level, it is evident that any two (or more) conceptually discriminable things may be logically subsumed under some single, higher-level category or factor. Consequently, any theory is transformable into a single-factor theory in that it focuses, at least implicitly, on a conceptualizable "second-order" factor common to the domain of its lower-level concepts.

It is also clear that, on the empirical level, the term "single factor" does not as such denote the *data* yielded by a single set of observations. Empirically, the single-factor model implies that diverse or operationally independent sets of observations are the manifest or overt expression of a single, *underlying* or latent vector. Somewhat more technically, a single-factor model involves the assumption that a correlation matrix of all relevant measurements can be reproduced with the use of no more than one common factor.

Viewed in still a different light, Single Factor Theory may be said to premise a distinction between dependent and independent variables; it proceeds by examining *many dependent* variables in their relation to *one independent variable*. It thus takes as problematic the task of demonstrating the diversity of influences generated by this single independent variable and of showing that changes in any and all of the dependent variables can be traced to an antecedent change in the preferred independent variable.

Single Factor Theory thus construed obviously possessed both logical and empirical defects. Among the logical weaknesses was its failure to consider systematically the ways in which the assorted dependent variables mutually affected one another. It also ignored the *reciprocal* influence of the dependent variables, singly or in concert, on the independent variable. Empirically, single-factor theories waned because of their Procrustean impulses; as Talcott Parsons aptly puts it, they "had a notorious tendency to overreach the facts."[2] Stated technically, more than one common factor would be needed to reproduce the original matrix of intercorrelations.

Although a single-factor model is today regarded as indefensible by practically all Western social scientists, there seem to be at least two forms in which it still survives and is expressed incipiently in our work:

(1) There is a widespread tendency among sociologists to rest content with the demonstration that some theoretically interesting variable "makes a difference." If a proposed variable can be shown to "influence" various social and cultural patterns, it is often felt that this suffices to legitimate it as a conceptual innovation, even though (*a*) the proportion of the dependent variable's variance which is accounted for is left unstated, or even though (*b*) this may be small in comparison with the proportion of variance which is accounted for by other, already familiar, variables.

This prevalent theoretical tendency parallels the single-factor model in that it entails a commitment to some preferred variable which is treated as explanatory of various others, without explicating that it accounts for only some proportion but not all of the variance in the dependent variables, and without taking as *problematic* the residual variance in the dependent variables, that is, the variance *not* accounted for by the preferred independent variable. Essentially, the effort here is to "justify" some general orientation and to demonstrate that a certain "interesting" variable can be ignored only at the analyst's peril. The researcher's interest is in the

---

[2] Talcott Parsons, *Essays In Sociological Theory Pure and Applied*, Free Press, Glencoe, 1949, p. 24.

independent variable and in *legitimating* its place in some theory, rather than in *accounting* for some problematic pattern or dependent variable.

(2) A second way in which remnants of the single-factor model are still visible in theorizing is in various forms of "sociologistic" analysis. The classic example of this is commonly held to be Durkheim's dictum that "social facts must be explained by social facts" or that "society is a reality *sui generis*." In more recent times, the polemical tendency to counterpose "cultural" against biological explanations of human behavior seems to be a similar, implicit form of single-factor theorizing. This also seems to be true of the current tendency of some sociologists to focus exclusively on "social systems" to the neglect of biological, climatic, ecological, or technological influences on behavior.

Pressure toward a single-factor model apparently intensifies when the analyst strives to establish a charter legitimating the independence of some social science—be it sociology or anthropology—just as much as when he is subject to extraneous compulsions of an ideological character.

Such pressures are, of course, most intense in the earlier, more embattled phases of a social discipline. When these pass and the discipline is more securely institutionalized, its claims tend to be less imperialistic. At that point "they refuse to be drawn into the position . . . of maintaining that *everything* about human behavior must be explained by the organization of social institutions, or of assuming that even differences in the natural endowment of men must be denied as a fact in order to lend seeming support to the sociological approach. . . ."[3]

Multiple Causationism was one of two major reactions to the manifest shortcomings of Single Factor Theory. In opposition to it, Multiple Causation counter-affirmed that any social or cultural phenomenon was produced by many factors rather than one. Multiple Causation focused on the diversity of contributants to a single out-

---

[3] Foreword by Robert K. Merton to Hans Gerth and C. Wright Mills, *Character and Social Structure*, Harcourt, Brace, New York, 1953, p. viii.

come and sought to identify the various independent variables producing one kind of event. While the Single Factor model worked with one independent variable and many dependent variables, the multiple causation model typically used *many independent* variables and *one dependent* variable.

In this way Multiple Causation lent greater "realism" to theory and research. Its underlying metaphysical pathos was more congenial to the liberal intellectual who, as liberal, sought a compromise between competing single-factor theories and who, as intellectual, was suspicious of the oversimplification and partiality of any one of the single-factor theories. The defects of Multiple Causationism were, however, substantial; indeed they were the mirror-image of those manifested by the single-factor theories. Multiple Causationism often entailed the successive study of the effects of various independent variables, taken one at a time, on one dependent variable. To this extent, Multiple Causationism failed to consider the ways in which the several independent variables affected one another, and neglected the reciprocal influence of the single dependent variable on the several independent ones.

Moreover, from the standpoint of the logic of science, Multiple Causationism sometimes had impulses at variance with the canon of parsimony, tending to the needless proliferation of independent variables. It sometimes failed to consider whether the independent variables it added really increased the proportion of variance accounted for in the dependent variables. It often ignored the possibility that the several independent variables used were simply outward indications of a much smaller number of underlying common factors or that they were but different measures of one and the same thing.

Functional Analysis, like Multiple Causationism, was in part born of a polemic against Single Factor Theory. Functionalism rejected the single-factor view that, within a given domain, there was some one variable that was inherently an independent one, and looked upon all variables as being both dependent and independent. It conceived of human groups as systems composed of parts which were interdependent and mutually influential, viewing each variable as both "cause" and "effect" and as linked to all others in the system. From this standpoint, changes in any one part of the system are seen as yielding far-ramifying consequences and as requiring interpretation in terms of all the other variables and the system as a whole.

Toward a Stratified System Model

Polemic commonly breeds overstatement, and it is surely overstatement to suggest that all variables in a system are *equally* involved in the system or equally influential in determining the state of the system or any of its parts. Merely to assert that two parts are interdependent begs the question of whether they are equally so; it ignores the problem of whether each is equally "functionally autonomous"—i.e., has an equal probability of survival when separated from the other.[4] What seems to be needed in place of this strategy of analysis is a different kind of model, a "Stratified System" model which will methodically note that even within a system of interdependent parts, not all elements are equally interdependent and that some have a greater, and others a lesser, degree of autonomy or independence. Despite the substantial progress of two decades led by Robert Merton and Talcott Parsons, it does not appear that functionalism has moved beyond the "interdependence" postulate described previously. This postulate has never been rescinded or significantly revised; it has only been forgotten. Functionalism today still rests upon a vague and dubious assumption of system interdependence which ignores the question of the differential influence of system elements.

The functionalist's system-postulate had an important implication for his image of cultures and societies. From the perspective of functionalists such as Radcliffe-Brown and Malinowski, emphasis was to be placed on the *integration* of societies and on the manner in which

---

⁴ This is discussed more fully in Alvin W. Gouldner, "Reciprocity and Autonomy in Functional Theory," in L. Gross (ed.) , *Symposium on Sociological Theory*, Row, Peterson, Evanston, 1959, pp. 241-270.

their various parts fused to form a quasi-organic whole. This viewpoint was advanced in opposition to the so-called "shreds and patches" conception of culture, presumably held by anthropologists such as Kroeber, Lowie, and Benedict, in which a specific culture, e.g., North American civilization, is seen as a hybrid possessing traits Germanic, Latin, Palestinian, Abyssinian, Phoenician, and Grecian in origin. In the latter view, cultures are not so much "organismic" as they are "composites," i.e., in Kroeber's quantitatively sensitive statement, "more or less fused aggregates of various origin, ancient and recent, native and foreign,"[5] some of which are more or less stationary, long-persistent, and slowly changing, while others are more rapidly diffusing and changing.

As in other polemics, the contestants allowed their differences to overshadow their similarities. It is clear that a view of culture as a "composite" converges with a view of society as "organismic" in that both are seen as some sort of systemic whole. The difference between the schools was not so much between those viewing culture as a mere aggregate of disparate elements—like a pile of debris—and those seeing society as a smoothly integrated organism. Clearly Kroeber, for instance, saw the element of mutual *adaptation* among ecologically adjacent traits, while, conversely, Malinowski sensitively explored the *conflicts* intrinsic to certain primitive kinship systems, even as Radcliffe-Brown enjoined a study of "dysfunctions."

At bottom, their debate was implicitly concerned with the question of the *degree* of integration or functional unity of the parts constituent of cultures or societies. Moreover, in some measure their debate often involved imputations about different things; functionalists typically stressed the integration of *societies*, while nonfunctionalists typically minimized the integration of *cultures*, and were often more interested in the history of concrete cultural items. If what was implicit in this controversy had been made explicit, the next fruitful steps could have been taken, that of asking which socio-

---

⁵ A. L. Kroeber, *The Nature of Culture*, University of Chicago Press, Chicago, 1952, p. 57.

cultural elements were more and which less integrated with others, or which elements were more influential than others.

In considering the question, as we will here, of which parts of a sociocultural system are relatively more influential, we can hardly fail to notice that numerous social scientists have repeatedly proposed convergent answers. A long line of social theorists from Saint-Simon through Marx, Ogburn, and anthropologists such as Childe, White, Steward, and Goldschmidt have, although stating their nominations variously, commonly stressed the influence of technology.

Despite the variety of ingenious philosophical, theoretical, and historical refutations trained against this hypothesis, it arises from the ashes of criticism again and again. Indeed, one still finds modern, heterodox thinkers such as E. H. Carr calmly turning their backs on this century-long controversy and blandly beginning their analysis by asserting, "Experience shows that the structure of society at any given time and place, as well as the prevailing theories about it, are largely governed by the way in which the material needs of the society are met."[6]

Few other factors are given anything like the recurrent mention afforded technology. One of these is the "family." While the sense in which this is proposed is not always clear still, it is not uncommon to find statements such as this in anthropological works: "The basis of every human society, from the most primitive to the most complicated, is the family. There is no form of society known to us of which this is not the case. . . . Kinship with them [i.e., in "small tribes"] dominates the whole scene of human relationships and activities, whether these be of a more restricted family nature or of a wider tribal or political one."[7]

Another factor, often closely associated with an emphasis on the importance of family because of the latter's socializing significance, is one which has been discussed variously under the rubric of the "role of ideas in history" and stresses the role of moral beliefs, val-

[6] E. H. Carr, *The New Society*, Beacon Press, Boston, 1959, p. 19.
[7] John Layard, "The Family and Kinship," in E. E. Evans-Pritchard *et al*, *The Institutions of Primitive Society*, Free Press, Glencoe, 1954, pp. 50-51.

ues, and norms. Its nineteenth-century expression is crystallized by Comte, passes through Durkheim, and is emphasized by Max Weber; this dimension has also been stressed in recent decades in the sociology of Talcott Parsons. In the latter case, however, since this dimension is located in a theoretical structure which is predominantly functionalist, its claims to predominance and precedence over others have not been quite so explicitly advanced, although it is unmistakably assigned special importance.

Both functionalists and cultural relativists alike have sometimes maintained that, while certain factors may be important for certain types of societies, there is, nonetheless, no reason to suppose that any one or several factors will be a primary influence in all. For example, it is sometimes suggested that while technology may be a primary influence in modern societies, it may not be as significant in traditional, folk, or "sacred" societies which do not prize rationality and technology as do we. In this context, the study of the relative influence of technology in "primitive" societies, such as those in our sample, assumes a special interest. For should technology be shown to have particularly potent influence, even in these societies, then it would seem reasonable to expect that it would have no less a role in industrial societies and may therefore be a factor relatively important in all. In any event, once having raised the question of the relative magnitudes and influence of different parts of the sociocultural system, we could not help being curious about what our data would indicate concerning technology.

We have suggested that, in polemical reaction to the weaknesses of single-factor theory, functionalism counterposed a stress on the *system* of variables as such. In taking the system of variables as problematic it focused on a diversity of mutually influential variables but ignored the differing extent of their influence.

Since they imply a *quantitative* difference between two or more factors in determining a given outcome, factor theories could not be given rigorous testing except in statistical or mathematical terms. It was in attempting to avoid these that functionalists were led into asserting the triviality that "everything affects everything else." For this, at least, provided a basis for empirical research with qualitative if not with quantified data. Earlier functionalists were constrained to make a vague affirmation of the "interdependence" of social parts, and to explore this qualitatively, because they lacked the statistical tools needed to determine which parts of the system, if any, were more and which less influential. Today, however, mathematical and statistical developments may be on the verge of making this possible and have, therefore, encouraged us to reopen this dormant issue and to propose an alternative to diffuse functionalism which we call the "Stratified System Model."

A Dilemma of Modern Ethnology

Without doubt functionalism has been one of the main *intellectual* forces in recent anthropology, another being cultural relativism. The first has led to painstaking studies of specific societies with a focus on the organization and integration of their component parts. The second, cultural relativism, induced heightened awareness of the diversity of cultures and of the need for a wide sampling of societies. Under the urgings of both these forces, "holistic" knowledge about individual societies was deepened while the number of societies studied was increased.

Ironically, however, this very cumulation of data creates an embarrassment of riches for the would-be builder of theory. There is scarcely any theory which is not lent seeming support by judicious illustrations selectively drawn from this treasurehouse of data. Conversely, there is no theory which is not seemingly controverted by the selection of equally partial data. The abiding problem is how this growing mass of data may either be mobilized as a whole, or else somehow reduced to manipulable essentials, so that it may be systematically brought to bear on theory.

More specifically, our dilemma is this: We must usually choose between (1) studying many variables in one or a few societies, or (2) studying and comparing many societies in terms of a few variables. Given the traditional methods, it is usually impossible to do both. Consequently, research, even at its best, commonly tends to take one of two courses. In one of these there is an intensive ethnographic account of a single society, with either an implicit or an explicit backdrop of impressionistic comparison to one or two other societies. In the other, there is a comparison of many societies in which, at most, two or three variables are treated *simultaneously*. Examples of the latter are the classic work of Hobhouse, Wheeler, and Ginsberg, or the more recent efforts of Murdock and his associates. While possibly the last is based on better data from a larger sample, it still uses much the same methods of statistical analysis as its famous predecessor.

Truly *systematic* cross-cultural comparison is as rarely found in practice as it is commonly extolled in principle. There are few if any men who have done field work in, and know at first hand, more than a half-dozen distinct cultures.

It has become increasingly evident that no single social scientist today can mobilize the immense body of data available if he uses the usual methods, whether quantitative or qualitative, of current research. It grows increasingly obvious that commitment to the principles of cross-cultural research can today be given only lip service unless we extend our methods to include modern statistical techniques and use, in particular, some form of multivariate analysis. Systematic cross-cultural comparison currently requires methods allowing the simultaneous analysis of a large number of "traits" studied in a large sample of societies.

The Use of Factor Analysis

In the study that follows, we shall attempt to apply one statistical method, factor analysis, to the problem of handling simultaneously a large number of traits in a large number of societies. Briefly outlined, factor analysis starts by determining the correlation of each variable with all others. Working with this matrix of correlation coefficients, factor analysis seeks to identify a multiplicity of items or traits which cluster together, forming a number of subsystems within the larger whole. Stated differently, factor analysis provides a basis for identifying the latent dimensions under-

lying a cluster of items. Furthermore, by indicating which items are
most highly "loaded" on—i.e., associated with—an underlying dimension, it may provide a means of selecting a parsimonious measure of
the dimension, thereby allowing many measures to be represented
by a few.

It may be that factor analysis can provide a set of measures or
operationalizations permitting a more formal approach to certain
important questions of system analysis. For example, by permitting
us to determine the items which share common variance with others
in a domain, it may enable us provisionally to bracket off the boundaries or identify the components of a system; it may permit us to
measure the "systemness" of a domain by estimating the amount of
common variance extracted by factors found in it. Or we might regard the factors themselves as delineations of the component subsystems and use the correlations among the oblique factors as a basis
for computing measures of the differential interdependence or functional autonomy of a subsystem. This will be discussed further in
Miller's methodological addendum. For the most part, however, our
interest here will be directed to identifying the differential magnitudes of the factors, to measuring the varying degrees of association
they have with one another, and to attempting various approaches
to the question of the differential influence or power of the several
factors.

At this point we should suggest somewhat more clearly what we
have in mind in talking of the relative "influence" of different factors and, especially, what kinds of operationalizations will be used
to gauge this within the limits of the synchronic kind of data to be
used here. Several different strategies will be considered; here, how-
ver, we need only give a relatively brief indication of them, since
they will be discussed in greater detail at a later point.

One method entails use of multiple regression techniques. We
will, in this connection, score each society in terms of each of the
factors which are extracted and measure the extent to which any
one set of factor scores can be predicted by any and all of the others.
In doing this, we will exclude or partial out the effects of the others

and thus establish some basis for appraising the degree to which any one factor predicts *all* others and, therefore, has the relatively greatest predictive value for the *total* set of factors. Secondly, we will seek to appraise the relative influence of factors known to be related to one another by attempting to appraise the degree to which each is relatively autonomous. We will suggest that, among related factors, the most autonomous ones, that is, those which are composed of more highly integrated core elements, will have the relatively greatest influence. Finally, we will attempt to see what can be learned from a "second-order" factor analysis in which, instead of factor analyzing the original scores, we factor analyze the first set of factors extracted.

It should be added, if only parenthetically, that factor analysis would hold little promise as one possible solution to our problems were it not used in conjunction with a recent technological innovation, namely, the high-speed electronic computers. Without these, the complex computational procedures required by the statistic would make its application to the massive data impossibly time consuming and insufferably boring, however possible in principle.

Before turning to specifics, a candid warning must be given; this is more than an incidental *caveat* and is basic to the entire outlook of our work. It is this: our efforts are at best a provisional attempt to explore the feasibility of using factor analysis for the purposes mentioned above. The specific results obtained can be no better than the data used, the method of statistical analysis employed, and the skill with which it was applied. It is particularly incumbent on us to stress the problems and difficulties now inhering in factor analysis since many social scientists are still unfamiliar with it. Although there have been literally thousands of factor analytic researches completed, nonetheless considerable disagreement persists concerning practically every major step in the technique. For example, there are disagreements concerning the number of common factors that should be extracted, the methods of extraction, of estimating "communalities," and of rotating factors, the relative merits of "blind" rotation versus rotation to a hypothesized matrix, the relative merits of orthog-

onal and oblique factors, and, indeed, the very meaning of the factors themselves.

We take a pragmatic view of these issues, for we are neither cultish
adherents to nor compulsive opponents of factor analysis. While
such bland assurances rarely allay partisan passions, frankness requires us to acknowledge that we regard factor analysis as no more
than a tool to be used here for what it is worth.

We use factor analysis despite our awarenesss of its many present
shortcomings and the often heated controversies surrounding it.
We use it for several reasons: First, we believe it to be a statistical
model which helps us approach the questions in which we happen
to be interested and provides answers in ways proximate to the terms
in which we seek them. Secondly, we use factor analysis because we
sense that these controversies are signs of a healthy intellectual fer-
ment which carries a promise, already demonstrated in part, of con-
tinuing and cumulative improvement of the method. Thirdly, we
use factor analysis because alternative methods of greater rigor and
elegance—such as latent structure analysis—were not, at the time of
our work, computationally feasible. Fourth and finally, we use it
because we suspect that these better or different methods will produce results in great part consistent with our own. Until replications
of our work, with similar or other methods, are completed and their
results compared with ours, the last assumption remains an item of
faith, as yet neither proved nor disproved. In general, we are most
inclined to respect the rhetoric of replication; whatever the merits
or faults of our work, these will be most convincingly demonstrated
by later replications.

Sources and Nature of the Data

Ideally, the exploration of the problems mentioned
above should begin with data representative of all societies and all
sociocultural traits. It appears, however, that ours is not the best
of all possible worlds. Here, as at subsequent points in the research,
we were constrained to compromise in order to proceed. This was
so, first, because only a fraction of the hundreds of societies which

now exist, or once existed, have been studied. Secondly, even societies which have been studied are not always fully comparable because traits focused on in one study were sometimes ignored in others. As an approximation of the information that would be ideally desirable, we employed data from the Yale Cross-Cultural Files presented in Leo Simmons' *The Role of the Aged in Primitive Society*,[8] which, at the time we made our analyses, contained the best sample available to us.

Simmons had worked with 71 societies (listed in our Appendix A) from many areas of the world. He had arranged their traits in two major categories: first, those bearing directly on the aged and aging, and, secondly, those of more general interest dealing with a broad variety of basic institutional areas. It was with the latter, a list of 109 traits, that we began.

Rather than dichotomously indicating the presence or absence of a trait in a specific society, Simmons had classified each on a four-point scale: (1) dominance, marked elaboration, or strong social importance in a given society; (2) persistence without dominance, moderate elaboration, or intermediate importance; (3) incipient presence, slight elaboration, or slight cultural importance; (4) absence or nonappearance of the trait when *definitely indicated* in the original sources. When there was no indication of the strength of a trait in a specific society, Simmons simply left it blank for that society. Our own correlational methods, however, required that all societies be given some measure of all the traits used; consequently, we were constrained to eliminate these "blanks." This was done in one of two ways. First, when a trait was blank for 1 to 19 societies, these omissions were replaced by the median value on that trait for all societies on which there was data. Secondly, when a trait was blank for 20 or more societies, the trait as a whole was eliminated from the correlation matrix. Forty-five traits were eliminated on this basis. In addition, seven traits were eliminated because their distribution was too sharply skewed, and one trait, "trade," was eliminated by

---

[8] Leo W. Simmons, *The Role of the Aged in Primitive Society*, Yale University Press, New Haven, 1945.

mistake. However, trade and several of the other eliminated traits were later introduced and will be considered in interpreting the results of our factor analysis.

The elimination of these traits, then, was not based upon our judgment of their theoretical importance. This does not mean, however, that theoretical considerations did not impress themselves upon and affect the sample. It is likely that recurrent lacunae in the data derive from theoretical assumptions shared by the researchers who had gathered the data originally. For it seems reasonable to assume that there is some relation between the frequency with which a trait was omitted and the degree of importance commonly attributed to that trait by anthropologists as a group. Specifically, it would seem that most of the traits we were constrained to omit by reason of the deficiency of data concerning them are likely to have been thought *less* important by the average anthropologist than most of those included in our study. We assume that anthropologists—like other social scientists— are more likely to ignore things they think unimportant, though data may of course be omitted for other reasons.

At any rate, at the end of this purely mechanical process of elimination, we were left with 57 statistically usable traits. These are listed in our Appendix B. Two more items were also added from Simmons' data. One was a measure of climate, classified on a three-point scale as follows: (1) severe climate, cold with long winters; (2) temperate, about equal winter and summer; (3) hot, little winter, much summer. The second item added had to do with the possibility of famine, which Simmons simply dichotomized as "danger" or "no danger" of famine.

We may well wonder just what is meant by some of the trait names used—for example, "agriculture" or "prevalence of warfare." Simmons has stated that the definition of each of the traits he used is the same as that presented in the *Outline of Cultural Materials*.[9] We must confess, however, that consultation of this *Outline* did not always dispel our uncertainties. Consequently, we were at times com-

---

[9] George P. Murdock *et al, Outline of Cultural Materials,* Human Relations Area Files, Inc., New Haven, 1950.

pelled to provide our own interpretation of a trait, and these may be at variance with the conceptions intended by those who originally classified the data. For this reason, and also because we had frequently encountered adverse judgments about the HRAF data from some anthropologists, we began our analysis with serious misgivings. We should also add, however, in anticipation of the report to follow, that the results produced by our factor analysis often made such manifest good sense, in terms of anthropological concepts and theories, that we came away, at the end of our work, with renewed respect for both the data and the manner in which it had been classified. It seems to us that since, on the basis of a purely mathematical analysis, many of the factors manifestly coincide with the concepts used by generations of anthropologists, this lends cogency to the statistical method used and seems to justify enhanced confidence in the Yale data.

After each of the 71 societies was coded in terms of each of the 59 traits or variables, each of the traits was correlated (using Pearson's r) with all of the others. The resulting correlation matrix, presented in Appendix C, was the basis of the factor analysis. As a next step, a set of factors was extracted from the correlation matrix, using the Centroid method of extraction and, we should add for the sake of technical completeness, using communalities of one. These centroid factors were rotated to simple structure using *three* different "analytic" criteria[10]—i.e., purely mechanical, hence replicable, methods rather than graphic or trial-and-error techniques of rotation. The presentation and interpretation of the resulting factors will occupy the major part of the next chapter.

---

[10] That is, the Varimax, Oblimax, and Quartimax solutions. These will be discussed shortly. For a description of the Oblimax see D. R. Saunders and C. Pinska, "Analytic Rotation to Simple Structure: Extension to an Oblique Solution," *Research Bulletin*, Princeton Educational Testing Service, 1954.

CHAPTER *2*

Four Dimensions of Primitive Society ~~~~~

For readers unfamiliar with factor analysis, a few elementary indications of how to "read" the tables that follow may be in order. Note that the "loadings" on some traits in a factor are larger than others. The loading is the correlation of a particular trait with the factor presumably underlying the cluster of traits presented in the table. Items with higher loadings are more indicative of the underlying factor than those with lower loadings. If a trait had a loading of, say, .99 or 1.00, it would be a near-perfect or perfect measure of the underlying factor. All traits are loaded in some degree on all factors, even if in extreme cases their loading is or approximates .00.

Note, also, that some loadings are positive and some negative. Whenever the sign of a loading is not given, the trait is positively loaded. When a factor has traits which are highly loaded, both positively and negatively, we may call it a bipolar factor. The extreme sides of a bipolar factor are contraries or opposites. Not all factors, however, need be bipolar. For example, psychometrists commonly hold that "intelligence" factors can only be unipolar in that the signs on all the constituent scales must all be positive, even if some are very low. Stated differently, there is, presumably, nothing like "anti-intelligence"; one can only have a relatively high or low intelligence. In general, a low loading does *not* indicate the opposite of a high loading of the same sign; it only indicates *less* of a correlation between that trait and the underlying factor than a higher loading.

TABLE I ～～ *Factor L: Lineality*

Item	V-loading (2)*	O-loading (6)†	Name of trait
36	824‡	926	Patrilineal inheritance
34	820	899	Patrilineal descent
38	801	934	Patripotestal family authority
37	744	838	Patrilineal succession
35	−741	−660	Matrilineal inheritance
47	635	563	Subjection or inferiority of women
33	−634	−485	Matrilineal descent
32	448	413§	Patrilocal residence

* V-loadings refer to the factor loadings obtained from the Varimax rotation. This is an "orthogonal" rotation, in that there is a mathematical requirement or artifact in the rotation maintaining all the vectors at right angles to each other. Less technically, none of the Varimax factors can be related to one another; all are independent of each other. The number in parentheses refers to the number of this factor in the Varimax Factor Matrix reported in Appendix D.

† O-loadings refer to the factor loadings obtained from the Oblimax rotation. This results in *primary* oblique factors; that is, these factors need not be independent of one another but may be related, positively or negatively, to each other. The number in parentheses refers to the number of this factor in the Oblimax Factor Matrix reported in Appendix E.

‡ Decimal points belong to the left of the first digit throughout. They have been removed for simplicity's sake.

§ Items with loadings lower than .400, whether negative or positive, are not shown in these tables but may be found in Appendices D and E reporting the various rotations.

The traits loading highest on Factor *L* and thus serving to define it are shown above. It is a bipolar factor, the positive end of which may be thought of as "father right" or patrilineality, while the negative end could be termed "mother right" or matrilineality. Our reason for using such terms as "father" or "mother right" is to stress that each side entails a multibonded linkage between generations. That is, each side entails more than the way in which members of a society reckon descent. For example, not only does the "father right" pole contain patrilineal descent, but it contains patrilineal *inheritance* and *succession* as well. Indeed, it is noteworthy that, on both sides of the continuum, inheritance is at least as important as the descent trait, if not more so, in defining the factor. As a whole,

therefore, the dimension is not limited to the actor's orientation to
the maternal or paternal lines; it also contains, in its loadings on
inheritance, succession, and authority, modes of the legitimate trans-
mission of power and wealth from generation to generation. If this
complexity is kept in mind, we may term the dimension as a whole
"lineality."

TABLE II ~~ *Factor SD: Sex Dominance, or Husband vs. Wife Right*

Item	V-loading (3)	O-loading (1)	Name of trait
41	−763	−994	Polygyny
31	741	898	Matrilocal residence
42	660	777	Monogamy
32	−635	−817	Patrilocal residence
4	402	438	Communal houses
52	x*	−507	Legendary heroes
27	x	−421	Government by restricted council

* Denotes that the loading is less than .400 on this rotation, though not on
the other.

As noted above, Factor *SD* involves traits having to do with residence; however, it is highly loaded on marriage forms as well. While
Factor *L* bears on the relations between older and younger generations, Factor *SD* involves the relations between members of the
same generation and, in particular, spouses. Factor *SD*, like *L*, is a
bipolar factor, the negative end of which involves patrilocality and
polygyny. Although it would be tempting to label the positive pole
as "matrilocality" and the negative "patrilocality," this might ob-
scure the fact that, on both sides, the factor is just as highly loaded
on the number of wives permitted a man. For this reason we might
term the negative pole as "husband right" and the positive as "wife
right," paralleling the terms used in describing the poles of the
lineality factor. At any rate, it is only by examining the implications
of this conjunction of marriage and residence forms that the factor
as a whole may be understood.

This conjunction suggests that we may have a kinship situation characterized at one pole by a *relatively* greater adaptation to the interests and pressures of women as wives and, at the other pole, by more adaptation to the interests and pressures of men as husbands. This, of course, assumes that men who live with their own relatives and can have several wives are more advantaged than those who must live with their wives' families and can have only one wife.

Clearly, polygyny and matrilocality are structurally incongruent (unless there is sororal polygyny). If a man has many wives, and if the rules of residence are matrilocal, there would, of course, be a problem of deciding with which of his several wives' families he should reside. There is, furthermore, a functional affinity between patrilocality and polygyny. In patrilocal societies a man lives surrounded by male kinsmen who can help him in work or war and to whom, in turn, he is similarly obligated. If he is married to one woman, the claims of his family of procreation may compete more strongly with those of his family of orientation. Married to several, his affective bonds with each are likely to be less intense and the demands that each can impose on him somewhat weaker. This would seem all the more probable as the wives mutually compete on behalf of either their children or themselves. Thus polygyny seems more functionally compatible with patrilocality.

What of the reverse pattern—how is patrilocality functional for polygyny? One possibility is that patrilocality facilitates war, from which plural wives may be won as booty and which also provides other booty that may be converted into bride price. Another familiar possibility also presents itself. That is, the jingle holds, "hogamous-higamous, men are polygamous, higamous-hogamous, women monogamous." This implies a "natural" differential in the sexual impulses of men and women; presumably, men want more sex than one woman is usually willing to provide, while women presumably have weaker sexual appetites than men.

We do not know the extent to which this is an ethnocentric projection of Western experience rather than a truly universal pattern. It is, however, at least consistent with the fact that polyandrous societies are far more rare than polygynous ones. But this same empirical generalization can be accounted for by another assumption, namely, the usual situation of male dominance. That is, there need be no difference in the "natural" sexual appetites of men and women, but, rather, a greater ability of males, because of their dominance, to satisfy their sexual impulses. This, too, makes an assumption about the impulses "natural" to mankind, though one rather different from that above. Here the assumption is that neither men nor women are "naturally" monogamous, although this is not necessarily at variance with the previous assumption.

The most cogent interpretation of this factor still seems to be that suggested initially—namely, that the factor as a whole is indicative of the *relative* positions of men and women, one pole denoting relative male advantage, the other relatively greater female advantage. Stated somewhat differently, this factor may be regarded as a measure of the degree of male dominance. One side of the dimension would indicate a comparatively "high price" or exchange value placed on women, while the other indicates that women are comparatively less highly regarded. What Murdock writes of conditions conducive to patrilocal residence in particular might be said to characterize this factor as a whole; i.e., it is indicative of anything "in culture or the conditions of life which . . . enhances the status, importance and influence of men in relation to the opposite sex. . . ."[1]

Whatever else may be said about Factor T, it is obviously highly loaded on traits quite different from those salient on either of the other two. Traits such as pottery, grain for food, mining and smelting of metals, weaving, and agriculture strongly suggest that the factor involves the *level of technology*, and perhaps particularly a neolithic technology. Factor T manifestly coincides with Childe's stress on the strategic significance of grain cultivation and pottery as two of the defining characteristics of the Neolithic Revolution. The significance of agriculture scarcely requires comment, but potmaking perhaps is less obviously significant, to sociologists at any rate, and deserves some discussion.

---

[1] G. P. Murdock, *Social Structure,* Macmillan, New York, 1949, p. 206.

TABLE III ~~~ *Factor T: Level of Technology*

Item	V-loading (1)	O-loading (9)	Name of trait
16	760	1493*	Pottery
11	705	1135	Use of grain for food
28	696	726	Prevalence of war
14	654	762	Mining and smelting metals
20	577	x	Slavery
13	551	512	Domesticated animals other than herded
18	546	615	Weaving
22	450	620	Money or a standard medium of exchange
10	442	535	Agriculture
29	427	x	Codified laws
17	x	693	Basketry
58	x	−656†	Climate (is warm)
52	x	−604	Legendary heroes
9	x	597	Herding
8	x	−572	Fishing
32	x	−499	Patrilocal residence
31	x	453	Matrilocal residence
49	x	425	Postmarital sex restriction on women
46	x	421	Difficulty of divorce for women

* In Oblimax rotations factor loadings can be larger than 1.0.
† Negative sign denotes that there is little winter and much summer.

It is, says Childe, "only in neolithic times that pot-making is attested on a large scale. . . ."[2] Childe emphasizes the association of pottery with certain basic developments in human powers. The potter's craft was a relatively complex one, involving an appreciation of various distinct processes and some of the earliest uses of chemical changes. In this respect, of course, pottery manifested the growth of men's instrumental capacities, being indicative of their developing dominion over nature and of a heightened capacity to mold it to their own purposes.

[2] V. G. Childe, *Man Makes Himself*, New American Library, New York, 1953, p. 76.

The development of pottery, it may be conjectured, also facili-
tated the occurrence of vital changes in man's conception of both
external nature and himself. For it provided a dramatically evident
exercise of man's control over nature and was a symbolically suitable
expression of a culminating growth of man's powers. This is all the
more likely because pots emerged in association with the cultivation
of plants and cereals, and were used to store, transport, and cook
them. Strange as it may sound, then, pot-making may have contributed importantly to the slow growth of human beings' conception
of themselves as artifactors, by making them increasingly aware of
and confident in their own instrumental powers. For, as Childe
says, "Building up a pot was a supreme instance of creation by
man."[3]

A distinctive characteristic of the potter's materials is their plas-
ticity, which creates problems quite different from those engendered
by chipping an axe. The potter must be able to create and select
alternative designs and forms, many of which might be instrument-
ally suitable. Potting thus constrains men to make aesthetic choices
and permits a greater latitude for play. It enhances and symbolizes
man's ability to impose his forms and designs on nature, as well as
his capacity to satisfy other needs. Thus pot-making is a unique
mixture of the instrumental and the expressive, of the utilitarian
and the symbolic, of work and play, of technology and art.

Pot-making, compared to agriculture, was completed in a relatively *brief* span of time and resulted in a stable embodiment and
externalization of men's plans, the pot itself. Thus men could see
what they had wrought, and could see that it had been wrought by
them. It would seem that this must have had significant consequences
for men's self-images. Man was now not only increasingly in control
of nature but also, and quite distinctly, increasingly *aware* of himself as an active controller of nature. To that degree, then, potting
heightened men's conception of themselves as *authors* of things and
thus, in effect, as persons.

---

[3] *Ibid.*, p. 79.

This line of analysis is, however, somewhat tangential to our central point, namely, that Factor T is indicative of the level of technology. The question of whether this factor may properly be regarded as indicating the level of technology deserves more careful examination; for technology is a variable central to the theoretic interests with which we began, and it is therefore important to be sure that Factor T can be regarded as "technology."

A Validation of Factor T

How, then, can our interpretation of Factor T, as "level of technology," be validated? Two possibilities suggest themselves. One is to determine whether societies' scores on this factor correlate with other social patterns in a manner consistent with the assumption that Factor T measures the level of technology. That is, we can ask if other social patterns customarily correlated with the level of technology also correlate in *this* instance, and in the predicted directions, with societies' scores on Factor T. Secondly, in order to validate our interpretation of this factor, we can attempt to determine whether our measures of it correlate positively with measures of the level of technology which were *independently* formulated and employed by other researchers.

In either case, what we required were individual scores for each society on Factor T. These were secured in terms of the *oblique* version of Factor T, rather than with the orthogonal version. (The reason for this was, of course, to allow us later to secure correlations between Factor T and other oblique dimensions; obviously, if societies' scores on orthogonal dimensions were used there could be no correlation among them.)

Returning to the first method of validating our interpretation of Factor T: If, as we suspected, this factor is an index of the level of technology, then we would expect that three traits, not included in our factor analysis, will be positively correlated with it. These traits are (1) written language, (2) trade, and (3) hereditary castes and classes. We would ordinarily expect these three traits to be positively correlated with the level of technology; consequently, if this occurs here, our inference that Factor T is indicative of the level of technology tends to be confirmed. We therefore turn to the relation between each of these traits and the societal scores on the oblique version of Factor T.

Forty-two societies were already scored for the trait "written language" in Simmons' sample. Only nine of these, however, have a written language, and these were separated from the others. The language data were then cross-tabulated with the societies' scores on T (which were dichotomized on the median). The results are indicated in Table IV.

TABLE IV ___ *Societies with high level of technology are more likely to have written language than those with low technology.*

Technology	Written language		
	YES	NO	TOTAL
High	7	14	21
Low	2	19	21
Total	9	33	42

Table IV reveals the expected association between Factor T and written language. This association, however, is even stronger at the extreme levels of technology: If, instead of dichotomizing societies by their level of technology, we divide them into quartiles, we find that *none* of the ten societies with the lowest technological level has a written language. Conversely, half of the societies in the highest quartile of technology do have written languages.

A similar procedure was used in analyzing the relation between Factor T and trade, which Simmons had scored on 65 of the societies with which we worked. Since we had accidentally omitted trade from the correlation matrix from which our technology factor was extracted, we could now use it to check our interpretation of the latter. Table V indicates the findings thus secured.

Finally, the relation between Factor T and the development of hereditary classes and castes was analyzed, again in a manner similar to that above. Information concerning hereditary classes and castes

TABLE V ～～ *Societies with high level of technology are more likely to have a high level of trade than those with low technology.*

Technology	Extent of trade		
	HIGH	LOW	TOTAL
High	22	11	33
Low	10	22	32
Total	32	33	65

for 45 societies was available in Simmons; these were correlated with the societies' scores on T, providing the following table:

TABLE VI ～～ *Societies with high level of technology are more likely to have hereditary classes and castes than those with low technology.*

Technology	Development of hereditary classes, castes		
	HIGH	LOW	TOTAL
High	20	2	22
Low	9	14	23
Total	29	16	45

In sum, each of the three traits tends to be associated with T in a manner that would be predicted if we assumed that T was indicative of the level of technology.

A final test of our interpretation of T was made. In this, we sought to determine whether measures of T correlated positively with measures of the level of technology formulated independently by other researchers. This was done as follows: In their classic work, Hobhouse, Wheeler, and Ginsberg made an extensive study of what they term "stages of economic culture." They classified their sample of societies according to economic stages and, at first, arranged these in a Y-shaped model. At the bottom of the Y they place "lower hunters" and, above them, on the stem, "higher hunters." On the left arm of the Y, going from the bottom up, there is "agriculture" 1, 2, and 3. On the right arm, there is "pastoral" 1 and 2.

Later in their discussion, however, they abandon this Y arrangement for a simple unilinear order, as shown in Table VII. For our purposes, it is noteworthy that Hobhouse *et al* base their classification on the society's principal means of obtaining food and on the level of technology generally. As they state, "This classification does not depend on any theory of the order in which the several economic stages have arisen. It merely arranges the stages actually found in an order corresponding to the degree of control over nature and mastery of material conditions found in each."[4] Consequently, if T is indeed a measure of the level of technology, then there should be a positive correlation between our T scores and the classification given these same societies in Hobhouse's study. That there is such a correlation is manifest from inspection of Table VII.

T A B L E   V I I 〜 ***Hobhouse's Classification of Societies***

Technology	*lower hunter*	*higher hunter*	*1st agric.*	*1st pastoral*	*2nd agric.*	*2nd pastoral*	*3rd agric.*	*N*
highest quartile								
1	0	0	0	0	2	1	6	9
2	0	1	2	2	3	1	0	9
3	0	7	2	0	1	0	0	10
lowest 4	4	2	1	1	1	0	0	9
quartile								
Totals	4	10	5	3	7	2	6	37*

* Only 37 of the societies in our sample could be confidently matched by us with those classified by Hobhouse.

In sum, given the findings presented in Tables IV, V, VI, and VII, it seems reasonable to conclude that our interpretation of T, as level of technology, tends to be confirmed.

With the presentation of the two kinship and the technology factors, we are now assured that all but one of the dimensions relevant to our theoretical interests are represented in our factor matrix. The only missing dimension of theoretical importance is one which may be coordinated to or interpreted as "morality." What we are

---

[4] L. T. Hobhouse, G. C. Wheeler, and M. Ginsberg, *The Material Culture and Social Institutions of the Simpler Peoples*, London, 1915, p. 29.

seeking is not so much a dimension which measures an historically concrete morality, e.g., Confucianism, but, rather, one which is indicative of certain of the more generic features common to *various* forms of morality. We believe that the next factor may be such a one:

TABLE VIII ⁓ *Factor A: Apollonianism, or Norm-sending*

Item	V-loading (7)	O-loading (5)	Name of trait
51	707	1313	Elaboration of ceremony and ritual
26	545	836	Power vested in chief
57	540	570	Attractiveness of future life
50	510	933	Organized priesthood
44	−491	−824	Marriage by capture
15	462	x	Metals secured from outside
29	437	461	Codified laws
56	433	x	Elaboration of mortuary ceremonies
30	403	936	Authority vested in judges
27	x	678	Government by restricted council
13	x	−537	Domesticated animals other than herded
52	x	468	Legendary heroes
34	x	−444	Patripotestal descent
38	x	−407	Patripotestal authority

A first glance at the Varimax loadings might suggest that this factor was focusing on religion or magic. A closer look at these loadings indicates, however, that only two of these specifically involve religious or magical traits. Items 26, 29, and 30 all have to do with the centralization or organization of authority. Item 50 might therefore be interpreted in two different ways; that is, either as part of a religio-magical complex or as part of a centralized authority dimension.

Examination of the loadings on the *oblique* version of the dimension can only lead us to doubt further the validity of interpreting this as a religion or magic factor. Two items clearly denoting authority, 26 and 30, all have higher loadings on the Oblimax. Correspondingly, one item indicative of religious belief (57) has dropped considerably in rank, from third place on the Varimax to seventh on the Oblimax. Despite initial appearances, then, it does not appear convincing to characterize Factor A simply as a religio-magical dimension.

The key question is what, if anything, is there in common among the most highly loaded items—i.e., those manifestly religio-magical and those manifestly indicative of centralized authority. Various answers to this question seem plausible. The one to be explored here suggests that this factor is indicative of the development of an Apollonian culture, akin to that described in Ruth Benedict's *Patterns of Culture*. To develop this possibility, and to elucidate its meaning, we decided to return to the earlier and remarkable analysis of Apollonian culture made by Nietzsche.[5]

In doing so, we are unhappily aware that, at this point, we may lose some of our remaining readers. We may lose those who feel that tainted philosophers have no place in a pure social science, or those whose liberal values are offended by Nietzsche's seeming anti-Semitism, or those who simply cannot bear the presumably gross incongruity of juxtaposing philosophical poetry and statistical analysis. We sympathize with such dismayed reactions but ask that they be deferred until we have seen, and considered in some detail, whether Nietzsche's conception of Apollonian culture bears any correspondence to Factor A.

Nietzsche counterposes the Apollonian to the Dionysian and extracts their paradigms from an analysis of ancient Greek culture. In schematic outline, and using his own terminology as much as possible, these take the ideal typical form outlined on page 33.

Doubtless Nietzsche would be dismayed to read this emaciated version of Apollonianism. Nonetheless, it suits our purposes here by

---

[5] F. Nietzsche, *The Birth of Tragedy and the Genealogy of Morals*, translated by Frances Golffing, Doubleday, New York, 1956. See especially *The Birth of Tragedy*. We must take notice when a scholar of the stature of F. M. Cornford tells us that this study was of such importance that it "left the scholarship of a generation toiling in the rear." F. M. Cornford, *From Religion to Philosophy*, Harper, New York, 1957, p. 111.

The Apollonian Model	The Dionysian Model
1. freedom from all extravagant urges (p. 21),* no excess, "nothing too much" (p. 34)	1. a sense of "glorious transport," "rapture," "intoxication," "demoniac"
2. rejection of all license (p. 26)	2. "sexual promiscuity overriding... established tribal law" (p. 25)
3. stresses "cognitive modes of experience" (p. 34), reason, knowledge, and science	3. surrenders to "intuition" or "instinct" (p. 51)
4. hopeful, melioristic view of world	4. tragic view of world
5. activistic	5. "loath to act" (p. 51)
6. "the *principium individuationis*" (p. 22), "know thyself"	6. "The bond between man and man comes to be forged once more," "the vision of mystical oneness" (p. 23), surrender thyself
7. emphasizes the plastic arts (p. 19)	7. emphasizes the "non-visual art of music" (p. 19)
8. maintains a compensatory belief in gods that lived (e.g., the Olymians) (p. 28-30)	8. (?) acceptance of the "terrors and horrors of existence" without illusion (p. 29)
9. "It was not unbecoming for even the greatest hero to yearn for an afterlife." (p. 30)	9. acceptance of the dissolution of the self

* Page references are to Nietzsche, *ibid.*

codifying the key elements constitutive of this pattern. In effect, Nietzsche's profound historical insight produced an impressionistic, qualitative "factor analysis" of Apollonianism which has surprising conformity with Factor *A*. Indeed, there seems a visible convergence even in the details of the two.

For example, note the similarity between paragraph 8 above, a belief in gods who had lived, and item 52 in Factor *A*, legendary heroes. There is also a manifest convergence between paragraph 9, a yearning for an afterlife, and the importance of item 57 in Factor *A*, also stressing the significance of an afterlife. Finally, there is item 44, marriage by capture, which is, appropriately enough, *negatively* loaded on Factor *A*. Even if not to be taken literally, marriage by capture may well have symbolic significance consistent with the Dionysiac element of sexual license, as indicated in paragraph 2.

More important than any of these cultural details, however, is the most generalized implication clearly attributed to Apollonianism by Nietzsche. It is obvious that he thought its primary character involved *impulse control*, as indicated by the terminology of paragraph 1 above, which is constantly reiterated. This may well be the common latent dimension running through both the manifestly religio-magical items and those manifestly indicative of centralized authority. Both these institutions require impulse control, deferred gratification, affect inhibition, expressive discipline, or instinct renunciation to indicate some of the diverse ways in which this important notion has been named.

The successful performance of ceremonial and ritual tasks, as well as adaptation to structurally differentiated and specialized systems of authority, both require that the actor forego certain immediate opportunities for gratification; both require that he control his impulses on behalf of his specific (moral or instrumental) aims. In other words, in the presence of supernaturally sanctioned ceremonial or ritual requirements, or of secular political power, a person cannot do the "first thing that comes into his head" or "whatever he feels like doing." This would seem all the more likely to the extent that political and religious institutions are less differentiated from one another in these societies than in our own and where, indeed, political authority is often given a supernatural sanction. Under these circumstances the individual must control his impulses or be punished both by external authorities and by an internal censor which would make him suffer anxiety, guilt, or shame.

In this connection, Malinowski's theory of magic and religion seems most apposite. It was his central thesis that ritual served to mitigate anxieties in hazardous situations otherwise uncontrollable technologically. Men were thus enabled to continue performing their social roles and to go about their business. In other words, magic and religion help men control impulses that might otherwise disrupt the instrumental effectiveness or moral propriety of their actions. As noted by Homans,[6] this formulation entails no necessary contradiction with Radcliffe-Brown's thesis that the stereotyped demands of ritual may induce anxieties, for fear that the actor may accidentally deviate from their meticulous requirements. There is no contradiction between Malinowski and Radcliffe-Brown here because Brown claims that anxiety *results from* fear of failure to perform the ritual as required, while Malinowski holds that magical ritual *reduces anxiety* when (properly) performed.

More importantly, perhaps, the anxiety reduced by ritual differs from the anxiety generated by fear of deviance from ritual requirements. The former is a kind of "primary" anxiety; the latter is a kind of "secondary" anxiety, in the sense that it is in effect a substitute for the former. This substitution, however, is a significant one insofar as the environmental hazards evoking primary anxiety are not controllable. In effect, the use of ritual means that men have substituted a controllable for an uncontrollable danger by substituting a compensatory control over self for control over external nature.

Whatever else they do, ceremony and ritual have a morality-strengthening function; in Radcliffe-Brown's terms, they "solemnize" certain orientations to nature and other men. As such, they serve to reinforce the "superego," revitalizing its ability to impose controls upon moods and impulses. Stated in still other terms, both ritual and centralized authority commonly have, in Ragnar Rommetveit's terms, a "norm-sending" function, i.e., emitting and sanctioning norms; these, in turn, serve to regularize and make more predictable behavior that might otherwise be vulnerable to the vagaries of impulse. But there are, of course, different kinds of norm-sending mechanisms; and Apollonianism with its stress on ceremonial and ritual, the attractiveness of an afterlife, and the importance of an organized priesthood appears to involve a *supernaturally* sanctioned norm-sending system. We shall have more to say on this in our next chapter.

---

[6] G. C. Homans, *The Human Group*, Harcourt, Brace, New York, 1950, pp. 326 ff.

The Relation Between T and A

Certain other aspects of Nietzsche's concept of Apollonianism deserve further comment because they provide a basis for predicting its relation to T, the level of technology. Insofar as Apollonianism involves a stress on cognitive modes of experience and a hopeful, melioristic view of the world (i.e., paragraphs 3 and 4 above) we should expect it to correlate positively with T. (This expectation is strengthened if we recall the stress that T entails upon a plastic art, pottery, and if we note that it is in this respect similar to Nietzsche's notion of Apollonianism, as indicated in paragraph 7.)

A test of this can be made by determining the correlation between factors T and A, in their oblique versions. This was done by a method, programmed for the electronic computer, which ascertains the spatial relations among the factorial vectors by plotting their hyperplanes, rather than by correlating the estimates of the societies' scores on both factors. The correlation thus found was .76, which is an unusually high one for social research in general and factor analytic researches in particular. It would be naively optimistic, however, to assign any great reliability to the *specific* coefficient obtained. For our purposes, it suffices to suggest simply that there is a clear indication of a strong positive relation between factors T and A.

Further indications of the close relation between Factors A and T may also be derived from inspection of the first centroid factor, reported in Appendix F. Here we can see that practically all of the items salient on T are also salient on the first centroid. Further, four of the items salient on A are also highly loaded on this same centroid factor, while three of the other items salient on A have loadings higher than .3 on the centroid factor. It therefore seems clear, from this different perspective also, that A and T are highly and positively related.

To sum up: Our evidence suggests that *the higher the level of technology, the higher the degree of demanded impulse control or Apollonianism.*[7]

---

[7] This, of course, has a familiar ring to it, being reminiscent of Freud's hypothesis that civilization requires the renunciation of instinctual gratification.

CHAPTER 3

Conjectures on the Relation Between Technology and Apollonianism ‿‿‿

Although we were of necessity led far from the data previously reported, it would have been strange indeed had we not speculated on the conjunction between technology and Apollonianism, and essayed a conjecture to account for it. In what follows we report our speculations for what they are and for what they are worth. The reader uninterested either in this question or in its exploration by informal speculation can proceed directly to the next chapter without loss of continuity.

Our conjecture takes its point of departure from the fact that technological advance was associated with the development of a more complex and differentiated system of social stratification. As Table VI indicates, T is positively correlated with the development of castes and classes. Similarly, the core items in T are also individually correlated with the development of slavery and plutocracy, as well as with the growth of a money economy and a higher level of trade.

A money economy means, among other things, that simpler social arrangements based on reciprocity will be drastically modified, while the growth of trade suggests increasing contact with the different beliefs of other groups. With this diffusion of new beliefs into the group there is a corresponding decline in the feeling that the older beliefs are an unchangeable "natural" order of things. The viability of the older system of beliefs is also impaired by the growth of social stratification. For this means that different social strata will be affected differently by various events, whether natural or social, that they are no longer operating in the same social space, and that the sense of a common fate shared by all members wanes.

The increasingly differentiated life chances and the heterogeneous life experiences of people in different social strata contribute to the growth of diverging social perspectives; beliefs and values are no longer so uniformly shared by members of the society. Moreover, as the technology develops it is able to support larger numbers of people and the group tends to grow in size. This growth, together with increasing social differentiation, may be expected to heighten difficulties in maintaining social order, in maintaining the cohesiveness of the group and its effectiveness in realizing its goals.

Tensions and social conflicts between social strata grow, along with intensified sentiments of ambition as well as envy, greed, and other aggressive impulses. Since Apollonianism is associated with technology, and the latter with growing social tensions, it can scarcely be expected that Apollonianism will be associated with friction-free social relations. Indeed, to the extent that the impulse control required by Apollonianism induces cumulative frustrations, Apollonianism itself may be a source of aggression. Impulse control mechanisms may, therefore, create some work for themselves, heightening certain of the very impulses that it is their business to control.

Stated otherwise, it is likely that the Neolithic Revolution in technology disrupted the established normative structures in the societies experiencing it. It introduced new social circumstances which made the traditional norms less applicable and, hence, reduced the value of conformity with them. The increasing social differentiation also associated with the Neolithic Revolution increases the probability of patterned variations in the interpretation of and in the conformity given the traditional norms, reducing the consensus or agreement among group members. It is also likely to have reduced the effectiveness of the older system of controls—such as patripotestal authority—which was lodged in the kinship arrangements.

As if these threats to social order and cohesion were not enough, it is likely that they were then accompanied by an efflorescence of individuality or of the "modern self" which also contributed importantly to the same effect. This point seems of such theoretical and historical importance that it will be examined below in some detail.

Evolution of the Modern Self

Social differences tend to intensify personal differences, yielding enhanced *individuation*. With the Neolithic Revolution there are now more and larger differences among individuals and thus a greater likelihood that each can perceive himself as different from the others. The individual is therefore less likely to feel a "Dionysian" union with all others but is, on the contrary, exposed to pressures which, in the classical Apollonian commandment, impel him to "know thyself." There is a heightening of the sense of self and a new spirit of individuality.

Whatever else it may entail, "self" apparently involves at least the following elements or dimensions:

1. *A discrimination of differences, as well as likenesses,* between the discriminating organism and others. The world is increasingly divided into two orders, that which is termed "I," "me," and "mine," and that somewhat residual category of the "other." Such discrimination involves a classificatory process in which experienced objects are assigned to different categories, differently named. The classification of an experienced object depends on the perception of both differences and similarities between it and others. Thus the self not only contains "attachments" and "commitments" to certain objects, the me and the mine, but also entails beliefs concerning the way in which these are both like and unlike other things, not me and not mine.

2. *The discriminating organism also develops a sense of or belief in its own power,* a belief that it can influence, cause, or control things in a sphere around it. In short, it acquires a *conception of will.* Originally, perhaps, will is felt and experienced as a sacred power, that is, as a *mana,* the mana attached to the self. Originally,

perhaps, the sense of the will's power is protomagical, for wanting
something and controlling it are felt to be intermingled. In sym-
pathetic magic, for example, to have a clear image or representation
of something and, above all, to be able to name it, is to have power
over it. Since wanting something may entail having a clear image of
it or a name for it, then merely to want something may be experienced as a form of control over it; "wishing will make it so." For example, the self has but to command the fingers of the hand to move
and, without discriminable intervening processes, the fingers nor-
mally do move. Thus the self is experienced as having a special force
attached to it, the will, an entity which, like a genie, may be sum-
moned to do the more arduous labors of the self. Crucial, however,
to the commonsense notion of "will power" is the feeling that it is in
control not only of external but also of internal objects, that is, it
can control the *self*, as well as others. This, however, premises that
the self is distinguishable not only from external but also from other
internal processes. We therefore note that:

3. *The organism discriminates its discriminations;* it distinguishes
between times of alertness and times of quiescence, of shaped awareness and of formless nonawareness; there is an awareness that some
things are mine and others not; there is not simply the fact of attachment and commitment to objects but a knowledge of such involvements; there is not merely a set of beliefs concerning such
involvements but a scrutiny of them; there is not merely a self but
a contemplation of the self. Thus the self develops and entails self-
consciousness, becoming an object to itself.

Perhaps it need hardly be said that none of these components of
self is an all-or-none entity and that each is, rather, a dimension
along which variations in *degree* can occur. The question is not
merely whether or not people have "selves," for that they do have
them is implicit in the definition of the "person"; rather, the question is how *much* of a self they have and what contributes to such
variations in degree.

We have said that the development of self is a development,
among other things, of the organism's discriminating processes; in

particular, it entails perception of the differences and likenesses between the discriminator and the discriminated. It is not, however,
the likenesses but the differences which are problematic and of crucial importance in distinguishing the self from others. Which is not
to deny, however, that the self can become acutely aware of its differences from certain others when noting its similarities to still
others. For example, a fat person can become uncomfortably aware
of his girth when he is joined by a companion of similar size.

If men failed to discriminate they would, of course, make similar
reactions to different things, or different reactions to similar ones;
while this need not always be fatal, it commonly makes action less
effectual or economical. When the world becomes increasingly differentiated, as it has in the societies under discussion, men must
make increasing discriminations among things, and especially among
men, if they are to make appropriate and effective responses to their
environment.

Yet not all differences among things or men are equally problematic. There is a greater need to discriminate things which are functionally important, to see differences which make a difference and
which, in short, help the person to enhance or maintain gratifications or to avoid or reduce deprivations. It is especially when men's
"differences" lead them to "differ," i.e., to enter into contention or
conflict, that these are most likely to be perceived. It is when men
"differ" that they develop a heightened awareness of their "differences." It is when Ego demands things of Alter divergent from Alter's
inclinations, when there is a breakdown in the complementarity of
their mutual expectations with subsequent threats to mutual gratification, that the need to take stock and clarify the differences between
self and other becomes more urgent. The cumulation and organization of these perceived differences *with* others become our perceived
difference *from* others. The difference *between* ourselves and others
becomes introjected and experienced as a difference *in* ourself, that
is, as our "individuality." Thus, awareness of self is sharpened by
increasing social differentiation and by conflict with others.

The people with whom we interact are, in various parts and ways, introjected into ourselves. We see things and ourselves, therefore, from their perspectives, thus making them part of us. The contents of the self are, of course, derived from social interaction, and, therefore, some form of social interaction is necessary for self-development. Our discussion above has not denied this but has, rather, been concerned with asking what *kinds* of social interaction are conducive to the development of self.

To the extent that the people and the demands introjected in ourselves are alike and make uniform and consistent demands on us, the management of self is a comparatively simple process. Under these conditions, it is essentially a problem of adapting our "natural" impulses to the demands made by others. When these demands are consistent and highly uniform, they also appear to be immensely powerful. The demands of many uniform others appear as part of an ordained or natural order of things from which there seems to be neither escape nor appeal. One has but to recall S. Asch's experiments on group pressures and conformity to get a sense of the power with which an undivided "collective conscience" can smother and suppress individual resistance. Certainly even these pressures scarcely produce a robot-like conformity; but they do produce a relatively homogeneous response, at least as compared with that elicited by more complex and differentiated societies.

When the demands introjected into personality differ and entail conflicting or inconsistent perspectives, then internal tensions are exacerbated and some tension-reducing effort must be made. The personality experiences a need to compose these different demands or to take sides with one against the other. External or social differentiation thus intensifies internal or personal differentiation. Efforts at coping with such internal dissension, like those involving the management of interpersonal tensions, reduce spontaneity and induce a heightened awareness of self.

The more that the people and the demands introjected differ, the more the personality differentiation and the greater the development of multiple selves within the personality. There can then be a withdrawal from one part of the self because there can be a retreat into another stronghold of self, from which the former may be viewed and distinguished. It is possible to surrender one attachment sanely only when there are other selves to fall back upon. When the self need not take the role of a single, all-powerful "other" but can diversify its investments among various competing others, and when it can shop among various roles for a self to be taken, it develops a feeling for its own decision-making vitality, a sense of its power, and a heightened self-awareness.

Heightened interpersonal tensions intensify the discrimination of various parts of the self as well as inducing discrimination between stimuli which are felt to be "internal" and those felt to be "external." The self increasingly becomes an object to itself when its impulses are not reflexively in keeping with the other's expectations, and when it receives responses not completely in keeping with its own. The self grows in self-consciousness when it feels a difference with others and when it does not view itself exactly as others do.

As the group's beliefs and values are no longer so uniformly shared, the self is no longer faced with so united a social reality. Consequently, the demands of the group are no longer experienced as quite so irresistible. The self now acquires an increasing sense of its own freedom; it becomes increasingly aware of its own power. Another way of saying this is that, with the Neolithic Revolution, there was increased "anomie," a narrowing of the degree to which values are shared in the group and a loosening of their hold on the individual. Far from being an unmitigated disaster for society and individual, however, this new anomie ushered in and coincided with a remarkable efflorescence of the self. With the declining power of the traditional beliefs and the weakening of social cohesion came the increasing power of the person.

The self's sense of power and will are usually linked, as in the idea of "will power." Will entails a belief in the self's power, in the ability of the self to accomplish something in the face of resistance, either external or internal. Will is also a capacity to mobilize and focus energies on some delimited objective. If there is no conflict, either in the self or between persons, there is no need for will. The function of the will is to resolve conflict within and between people, by taking sides and establishing the dominance of one of the contending parties or forces.

The Neolithic development of technology strengthens the self's feeling of power by giving it increasing control over nature and greater practice in decision-making. With the growth of this sense of the self's power comes a growth of self-*regard*. (Conversely, the growth of self-regard provides added motivation and energies mobilizable on behalf of actions consistent with the view of the self.) As used here, self-regard is not identical with self-*esteem*, which is a pride in being or having a socially approved self. Rather, self-regard arises from the sense of the self's potency. Self-esteem depends upon social approval and is based upon the conformity of the self with certain group values. Self-regard, however, may be experienced when the self violates the expectations of others, when the self manifests a capacity to express distance from others and their demands rather than involvement with or attachment to them. That is, self-esteem derives from consensual validation, while self-regard derives from conflictual validation. Self-regard may be felt to the extent that the self conceives itself as having a field of autonomy (or "free will") which it may experience when it manifestly becomes something to be reckoned with, even if not approved by others. Self-regard may be experienced when the self can realize its objective despite others' resistance and when, therefore, it may be deviating from rather than conforming with socially current standards. Potency is in this sense an internal (perhaps cross-cultural) norm by which the self evaluates itself.

Validation: Consensual and Conflictual

There are at least two different ways in which the self can feel itself to be "real" or two senses in which it can feel "sure" of and validate itself: through feeling powerful in the course of conflictual validation or through feeling loved and approved in the course of consensual validation. The search for consensual validation, however, runs the risk of inundating the self, for it constrains the self to conform and to be like others, thus thinning down its own distinctiveness and blurring its identifiability. Without tensions with others, the boundaries of the self become looser and more permeable, the line between self and others grows wavery. Conversely, the maintenance of the self's boundaries through tension with others may exacerbate resistance and induce others to withhold consensual validation, thus undermining the self's convictions concerning its character and qualities.

It is partly because the life of the self requires some measure of tension with others that the maintenance of self is a costly business. And because it is energy-consuming the self must be periodically relaxed or surrendered, as, for example, in games, sleep, sex, or spontaneous sociability with others. It is in part because the self needs periodic consensual validation from others that its sense of separateness from them is painful and it must lower its boundaries occasionally. On the other hand, it is because there can be no self without some boundaries, no self without some differences from and with others, that the self sometimes seeks out and sharpens tensions with others. And, indeed, the more the self senses the pull of its own passive, boundary-forgetting impulses, the more it may lurch into aggression. The maintenance of the highly developed self entails an endemic rift between self and society.

There is, of course, at least one way in which the self may receive both consensual and conflictual validation, in an integrated and synchronized manner. This is through participation in group conflict. With the increasing social conflict postulated above, the individual is appealed to increasingly, asked to take sides, and has more opportunities to make decisions concerning his group alliances. These experiences are conducive to his sense of potency or self-regard, for those appealing to him to join their side in effect tell him that he *makes a difference*, thereby consensually validating his growing sense of self-regard. Once committed to a group involved in conflict, he receives *conflictual* validation of his self in relating to his group's common enemies and *consensual* validation from his own group for adopting their posture toward the enemy.

Thus the highly developed self, although a social product, is not a simple, *sociable* product. It is not wholeheartedly and single-mindedly committed to friendly cooperation with others. Rather the self requires for its very survival both cooperation and conflict.

In our discussion above, we have focused on the ways in which changes inherent in or associated with the Neolithic Revolution in technology accelerated the development of self. It has not been suggested that before this time men were devoid of self. The burden of our argument is that self should not be viewed as an all-or-none thing but that it is a *variable* of which there can be more or less and that, with the Neolithic Revolution, there was a good deal more of it.

To sum up thus far: with the waning of the older tradition and the growth of a more diversified and heterogeneous system of beliefs and values, with a more differentiated culture and social structure, came more differentiated and fully developed selves. With these, partly as cause and partly as effect, came increased tensions among groups and social strata, a greater capacity of the self to feel distant from the demands of the group, a growingly diffused strain in the relations between the individual and the group.

The new self intensifies the problem of impulse management not only because it is more individuated but also because its constituent impulses are more powerful; as indicated above, the new self has a heightened sense of its own potency. This intensification and diversi-fication of impulses heightens the problem of maintaining social order and cohesion, of adjudicating interpersonal differences, of controlling the mutual interference of persons and groups, and of synchronizing their various contributions to task performances. There seem to be essentially two ways in which this problem may be solved: by the utilization of power differences and/or through the development of a normative structure.

In the first instance, divergent impulses may be controlled by es-tablishing some system of dominance, by utilizing power advantages to punish interference from the less powerful, and by rewarding their compliance or acquiescence. Social scientists have, of course, been too long familiar with the costs and difficulties of this solution to consider them once again in any detail. Suffice it to say here that new coalitions may overthrow a previously established "pecking order"; in such coalitions several parties or groups, each of whom may be individually weaker than a stronger one, may, upon combining, muster strength sufficient to disrupt a previously established balance of power. It is also well known that the costs of surveillance in such a purely power-controlled system may be prohibitively high, for the behavior of the subordinated party is less predictable when it is not open to inspection. This seems especially likely in groups of growing size and complexity, such as those under discussion here.

Impulse Management and the Moral Order

The second basic strategy for coping with the social disruptions deriving from conflicting impulses—namely, development of a normative structure—entails a system of reciprocal moral beliefs (concerning what "should" or "ought" to be done in various circumstances) agreed upon or shared by the interactors. Given such a normative system, mutual interference is lessened because the behavior of both the weaker and the stronger parties becomes more reliable and predictable. This is so under several conditions: (1) Insofar as the norms are judged to be not merely expedient or useful but legitimate, right, and proper; they thereby facilitate selection of a course of action even when its consequences are doubtful or incalculable and reduce the time and costs of making a decision, individually or collectively. (2) Insofar as the norms are shared, or held in common, by the interactors; this conduces to a common definition of a situation in which there is greater complementarity, such that each is more ready to do for the other what the other expects him to do. Further, insofar as the norms are shared each will experience greater consensual validation, being more likely to feel that the norm, or action stemming from it, is right and appropriate. (3) Insofar as the rules are reciprocal, in the sense that they state the "rights" of both interacting parties, so that each has both "rights" and "obligations." The existence of a system of reciprocal rules in effect establishes an arrangement for an exchange of gratifications, each being ensured that he will get something in return for what he has given which will reinforce him to continue such giving in the future.

While such reciprocity contributes powerfully to the maintenance of social cohesion, it is not, however, the first line of defense against conflicting impulses. In other words, when a conflict of impulses occurs, when, for example, P wants *x* from O but O wants to do or give *y*, then, given an established system of moral norms, individuals will first scan it, seeking out the relevant rules to compose the difference. Appeals will first be made to the propriety of one course and criticisms will be leveled at the impropriety of the other. In other words, a challenged course of action is first defended by justifying it as consistent with a rule which both parties accept as legitimate and by impugning the moral character of other courses or of persons who espouse them. Only after this fails over some period of time should we expect recourse to the withholding reciprocity.

The probability that a rule will be accepted as a basis for the adjudication of conflicting impulses increases with the extent to which it is mutually defined as being morally right or morally obligatory. In turn, the diffuse and protean judgment underlying and evoking such a conception, a common latent meaning of "should," "ought," or "duty," is that the performance it demands is *not selfishly motivated*. A rule is commonly believed to be morally binding to the extent that it is believed *not* to be expressive of a purely selfish interest or partisan advantage of the claimant, or of those whom it endows with rights.

If the rule invoked to adjudicate conflicting impulses is felt by the claimee to be the arbitrary invention of the claimant, or if his claim is not defended by an appeal to an impersonal rule, the claimee will be more likely to feel that the claimant seeks a partisan, selfish interest to which he will not, therefore, accord legitimacy. He will, as a result, be less likely to submit to the claim, or if he does will be more likely to do so out of fear of the claimant's superior power, biding his time until he can either escape the latter's control or retaliate against it.

To be thought legitimate, therefore, a rule must meet one or more of the following conditions: (1) it must be associated with gratifications or benefits to the *claimee* as well as to the claimant; (2) it must be associated with gratifications to neither but to some third party whose claims are agreed to be legitimate; (3) it must be seen to entail disadvantages or deprivations for both, the claimant no less than the claimee. Often enough, however, it is difficult for actors to judge by direct examination the allocation of benefits yielded by the rules; for their net consequences may be obscured in a tangle of extended ramifications. Imputations about the allocation of benefits are, however, often made by examination of the manner in which the rule arose, or from the way in which it is believed to have been established or derived. The more that rules are thought to have been derived in a manner that avoids or dispels any suspicion of partisan benefit for certain individuals or groups, the more likely they are to be deemed legitimate in themselves. Certain imputed derivations of rules are evidently more consistent with a belief in their nonpartisan impartiality than are others.

Above all, this means that rules which were created (or are believed to be created) solely by those benefiting from them have the least likelihood of being defined as legitimate. "Democratic" systems of rule-making are, contrariwise, more likely to produce rules deemed legitimate because they minimize the suspicion that partisan interests have shaped the rules, since even those for whom the rules establish obligations were involved in creating them. Rules which are believed to be very old—traditionalistic normative structures— and thought to be a heritage of earlier generations may to some degree obviate distrust and suspicion of special advantage to those who are claimants under them, because they manifestly could not have created them. Rules deriving from some agency which is believed to be nonpartisan and impartial, vis-a-vis conflicting claims in the larger group, will also be more likely to be judged legitimate than rules deriving from some agency identified or believed to be allied with one of the contending parties. This, of course, is one reason why it is supremely important for the state to project and protect an image of itself as nonpartisan in relation to the contending interests within the larger society.

One of the most common rhetorics for communicating that the rules are suprapersonal is to claim them to be the gift of or superintended by the gods. To hold the gods to be the fount of morality implicitly denies that the latter derives from or gives advantage to the special interests of some social group. It is this that vouches for the "justice" of a morality held to be divinely ordained. It is not merely that violation of such a morality may be seen as a sacrilege provoking an inescapable nemesis, although this surely induces powerful motives for impulse inhibition and conformity with morality; attributing moral rules to a god who stands above human groups and their conflicting interests also betokens the impartiality of the rules, thereby infusing them with legitimacy and inducing men to give them willing obedience. That the gods themselves could be unjust is intrinsically difficult for the believer to accept, for then all would in any event be lost.

This analysis seems to be supported by findings recently reported in G.E. Swanson's *Birth of the Gods* (University of Michigan Press, 1960), an excellent study of the origins of religion. Swanson raises the question of the conditions under which supernatural control is believed, in primitive or pre-industrial societies, to be exerted over the moral relations of individuals. In general, Swanson holds that this belief arises where there is an increased strain in interpersonal relations and when social discord grows. In particular, he finds that belief in supernatural sanctions on morality is more likely when there are greater debt relationships, social stratification, and increased use of grain crops—a configuration of circumstances characteristic of our technology factor. Thus Swanson confirms what we had only conjectured above before becoming acquainted with his study, namely, that the supernatural sanctioning of morality, implicated in Apollonianism, is associated with growing social and interpersonal strains.

The main differences in our analyses seem to be these: Our interpretation seeks to specify the way in which a supernatural sanctioning of morality copes with the growing strains of an increasingly stratified society by viewing it as a way of communicating the non-partisan character of social norms, thereby making them moral; in general, we have attempted to set the entire problem of super-natural sanctioning within the context of more generalized consid-rations concerning a sociology of morals. Moreover, we have also sought to relate these growing social tensions to the development of the more individuated, self-conscious self, to the very "individ-uals" whose existence is premised by the notion of a "moral rela-tion." Further, we have stressed that these social tensions are linked to technological developments and have attempted to set this larger configuration in an evolutionary perspective, suggesting that it may be seen as part of the Neolithic Revolution.

The Apollonian Complex

In our interpretation, the Apollonian factor entails a complex of norm-emitting, legitimating, surveying, and sanctioning arrangements, emerging as an adaptive response to the intensified so-cial conflicts and growing problems of impulse management which were then occasioned by the growth of Neolithic technology, increas-ing stratification, and heightened individuality. There is in Apollo-nianism a development of norm-sending institutions such as ceremo-nial or ritual and of codified laws, as well as of groups and roles such as a powerful chieftainship, authoritative judges, a restricted council, and an organized priesthood bulwarked by beliefs in the attractive-ness of the afterlife.

One final question will be broached here. It would appear that the compliance with impulse control demanded by Apollonianism requires some sacrifice; impulse control entails a more or less costly renunciation of immediate gratifications. Why is this price paid? Several reasons suggest themselves. One, of course, has to do with the more effective power system which can systematically punish infractions. Another is the expectation of an attractive future life, which may be particularly important to those of heightened self-consciousness, insofar as the latter entails heightened anxieties about

death. The priesthood may be able to manipulate such anxieties to
strengthen conformity with the norms by giving assurances about
the future life, as well as by providing or denying ritual preparation
for it. Further, the growth of technology itself makes available, in
some proportion to its development, a growing set of rewards which
can, here on earth, compensate for the costs of impulse control.

These several inducements to impulse control would seem in part
to be functional alternatives and, in some degree, mutually substi-
tutable. It would seem that if one declines the others need to be
strengthened and, conversely, if one is strengthened the others may
decline without loss of impulse control and thus without ramifying
damage to the social system. For example, the power system may
decline in strength if the moral system and/or the technology are
strengthened. Similarly, it seems conceivable that both the power
and the supernaturally sanctioned moral system, here conjoined as
Apollonianism, may decline with a great growth in technology.

From this theoretical perspective the correlation found between
technology and Apollonianism need not and would not be expected
to continue into later epochs in which technology could supply
greatly increased rewards. (In brief, the relations between the factors may be historically limited and need not be present at all evolutionary "stages.") Indeed, it would seem that this is much of what
Durkheim had in mind when he said that, in modern industrial societies with their advanced division of labor, the "collective conscience" would no longer play the same potent role in maintaining
social cohesion as it had in earlier periods, and that organic solidarity would tend to replace mechanical solidarity.

This line of analysis may also imply that a concentration of Apollonianism, in various forms, may be especially needed as a "starting
mechanism" at the beginning of a major technological spurt or re-
organization, insofar as this entails a heightening of deprivations
or an initial sacrifice of traditional gratifications. Under these conditions, a concentration of Apollonianism may serve in effect as a
form of "deficit-financing," providing social controls during a period
when the new technology's rewards are not yet available to motivate

the new demands for impulse control. When and insofar as the increased rewards of the new technology are distributed it may be that Apollonianism is a less necessary source of impulse control and may slacken.

CHAPTER 4

The Relative Magnitudes
of the Factors ~~~~

Having indicated that kinship, technology, and Apollonianism (or norm-sending) appear as factors, we may note that the "star actors" have at least made their appearance. How important their roles are remains, however, to be seen. For our purposes, we need not be much concerned about the other factors; at least, we need not characterize them specifically to explore the problem in which we are interested. (Those interested in the other factors can find them in Appendices D and E.) Since we successively extracted ten orthogonal and eleven oblique factors in all, a relatively large number as such matters go, it seems likely that if there were any important competitors they could be found among the remaining factors.

We are now, therefore, in a position to return to the central issue with which we began: Which is the most influential factor, kinship, technology, or norm-sending? More specifically, what is the importance of these factors in relation to each other and in relation to *all* the others extracted? At this point we must consider the way in which the relative influence of a factor might be defined operationally, and we need operationalizations or measures that are in reasonable agreement with our notion of "importance."

One crude method might be to define "influence" as the proportion of variance which a given factor extracts from the total variance in the original correlation matrix. In this case, variance means the sum of the squares of all the factor loadings for each factor. This measure gives an indication of the extent to which the original matrix of correlations can be reproduced or accounted for by the factor in question.

We might assume that if technology is the most "influential" factor it will extract more variance than that extracted by any other factor. Using the method described above, Table IX indicates the (absolute) variance extracted by each factor. Column 3 reports the variance extracted by the factors secured through the Varimax rotation, while column 4 shows the variance extracted by factors secured through the Quartimax rotation, which will be discussed later.

T A B L E   I X ⟿ *Extraction of Variance*

V-Factor number	Rank Order	Varimax variance	Quartimax variance
1 (Technology)	1	524	629
2 (Lineality)	2	517	503
8	3	399	436
3 (Sex dominance)	4	355	388
7 (Apollonianism)	5	343	299
4	6	291	258
5	7	258	224
10	8	258	234
9	9	230	208
6	10	207	204

Column 3 indicates that technology does indeed extract more variance than any other factor, although exceeding Factor *L* by only a small amount. It may be, however, that the reason for this small difference derives from the kind of rotation, the Varimax, which is reported in column 3. The Varimax Rotation was developed by Henry Kaiser[1] in an effort to improve upon another rotation, the Quartimax.[2] It sought to overcome an interesting weakness in the

---

[1] Henry F. Kaiser, "The Varimax Criterion for Analytic Rotation in Factor Analysis," *Psychometrika*, *23*, 1958, pp. 187-200.

[2] For a description of the Quartimax see J. O. Neuhaus and C. F. Wrigley, "The Quartimax Method: An Analytic Approach to Orthogonal Simple Structure," *British Journal of Statistical Psychology*, 7, 1954, pp. 81-91.

Quartimax—namely, the latter's tendency to maximize the loadings
of some variables for some one factor while minimizing them on all
others. In contrast, the Varimax tends to distribute the variance extracted more equally among all of the factors, thus clarifying the
smaller factors but at the same time reducing the amount of variance extracted by the largest factor.

It is precisely this "weakness" of the Quartimax rotation, however,
that makes it interesting to us here. For if we want to know which of
several factors extracts the largest amount of variance, it may be that
the Quartimax can tell us this more clearly than the Varimax. Stated
differently, if we want to know which of a set of factors tends to be
the biggest and most general, extracting the largest amount of variance, the very weakness of the Quartimax may enable it to provide
a clearer answer than the Varimax.

In Table X below we present the loadings on the technology factor produced by the Quartimax rotation, comparing these with the
Varimax loadings on this factor.

T A B L E   X ⁓ *Varimax and Quartimax Loadings
on Factor T Compared*

Item	Varimax loading	Quartimax loading	Name of trait
11	705	805	Grain for food
16	760	769	Pottery
28	696	690	War
14	654	609	Mining and smelting metals
18	546	607	Weaving
10	442	569	Agriculture
20	577	543	Slavery
13	551	538	Domesticated animals other than herded
12	x*	475	Constancy of food supply
26	x	469	Power vested in the chief
1	x	461	Permanency of residence
29	427	451	Codified laws
15	x	410	Metals secured from outside
39	x	403	Plutocracy
17	x	401	Basketry

* x denotes a loading of less than .400.

As expected, the items with the highest loadings on the Varimax rotation tend to have even higher loadings on the Quartimax rotation. Moreover, there are now six new items, with loadings higher than .4, on the Quartimax factor. The variance extracted by this and all other factors secured through the Quartimax rotation is listed in column 4 of Table IX, presented earlier. There it can be noted that the *rank order* of the Quartimax factors, when arranged by the amount of variance each extracts, is almost identical with that of the Varimax factors.

Note, however, that the variance extracted by the technology Quartimax factor increases by almost 20% over the Varimax; this is a far greater increase than that manifested by any of the other Quartimax factors. While the variance extracted by T (1) is just barely larger than that extracted by L (2) in the Varimax rotation, the variance extracted by T (1) is about 25% larger than Factor L (2) in the Quartimax. What the Quartimax rotation suggests is that *if* there is any one factor clearly predominant over its nearest competitors it is the level of technology. Nonetheless, it should also be noted that even this factor accounts only for a fraction of the total variance extracted. From this it is obvious that a monistic theory which holds that technology, *by itself*, determines *all* other relations is simply wrong. These data do not, however, disconfirm but are instead consistent with a hypothesis that, of all the various factors influencing sociocultural outcomes, technology is *relatively the most important*.

The above, however, may be an unsatisfactory way of assessing the "importance" of different factors. This is so because the variance measure used shows the importance of a *factor* in accounting for the variance in a set of concrete *traits*; it may, therefore, be inflated by the particular and possibly unrepresentative sampling of traits used. For example, technology may extract more variance than other factors simply because there were more technology traits included in our data. (It remains an interesting question whether any concrete trait can be said to be part of Factor T, or any other factor, thus enabling us to draw a representative sample of traits, without prior factoring and solely on the basis of nominal stipulation.)

The previous measure of the relative importance of a factor is also unsatisfactory because it deals with the orthogonal factors, where we labor under the dubious restriction that the dimensions be kept independent of each other. Clearly, it would be preferable to have a measure of the relative importance of each *oblique* factor in accounting for the variance, not in the sample of concrete traits used, but, rather, in all the other oblique *factors*.

A crude gauge of this may be provided by determining the average correlation which any one factor has with all of the other ten. This is indicated in the table below:

T A B L E   X I 〰 *Correlation of Oblique Factors*

Rank	O-Factor	Mean correlation
1	5 (*A*)	.36
2	9 (*T*)	.35
3	7	.32
4	8	.26
5	3	.26
6	4	.23
7	11	.21
8	2	.20
9	1 (*SD*)	.19
10	6 (*L*)	.19
11	10	.17

This table does suggest that the kinship factors, *L* and *SD*, are much less implicated in the entire system of factors than are *A* and *T*; but it indicates no noteworthy difference in the degree to which *A* and *T* are involved in the system. Moreover, since the above table is based upon the use of the zero-order correlations, it may be that the relation between any two factors is masked or suppressed, with consequent distortions in the mean correlation coefficients reported and in the differential magnitudes revealed. One possible way of dealing with this is as follows:

Using the zero-order correlations among the primary oblique factors, we computed multiple regression equations for each of the eleven factors. That is, each of the eleven (primary) oblique factors was taken, one at a time, as the dependent variable, while the remaining ten obliques were treated as independent variables vis-a-vis that factor. Thus eleven multiple regression equations were computed, each containing a different oblique factor as the dependent variable.

Having the equations for all eleven factors, we may then make an imputation about the importance of each factor in accounting for any other factor. The relative significance of any one factor for the *entire set* of factors was assessed by summing its relative contribution to each of the ten equations in which they served as independent variables. (There are, of course, ten rather than eleven numbers to be summed because there was one equation in which each factor served as a dependent variable.) That is, the betas (standardized partial regression coefficients) of each factor in each of the ten equations in which it served as an independent variable were summed. This then served as an index of the relative amount of variance that each factor influences in all the others. This is summarized in Table XII.

TABLE XII ～～ *Influence on Variance*

Rank	Score (sum of betas)	Factor No.
1	2954	9 (*T*)
2	2471	5 (*A*)
3	2295	7
4	2018	11
5	1848	4
6	1664	2
7	1331	1 (*SD*)
8	1250	8
9	1214	3
10	1204	10
11	1157	6 (*L*)

From this set of scores it appears once more that technology is the single most influential factor, in that it predicts more of the variance in all of the other factors than does any other single factor. Close behind it is Apollonianism, while well after this are sex dominance and lineality, which predicts the least variance of all factors.

Still another way of attempting to gauge the relative influence of *T* and *A* may be as follows: If we may think of each factor as a system-like entity, rather than simply as a linear extension or dimension, and, more narrowly, if we think of a factor as akin to an "atomic" system, we are led to questions about its "core" or "nucleus" and its internal relations and stability. The core items of a factor may be defined as those variables which are most highly loaded on it, beyond an arbitrary level, and are, therefore, the best or purest measures of the factor. Here we shall use the Oblimax factors to explore and compare the core structures of T and A. The core items of A and their correlations (r's) are:

TABLE XIII

Item No.	51	30	50	26
51	—	343	397	321
30		—	198	357
50			—	405
26				—

The core items of T and their correlations are:

TABLE XIV

Item No.	16	11	14	28
16	—	625	480	502
11		—	444	407
14			—	425
28				—

The above two tables indicate that the internal structures of these two cores differ substantially. The average correlation in T's core is notably higher than that in A's core. In fact, the lowest r in T's core is higher than the highest r in the core of A. Stated differently, the variance in any one of T's core items is more strongly controlled by its own, other, core items than is the variance in A's core. T thus has a more closely integrated core, a tighter or more mutually interdependent set of core items, than A. It would therefore seem less permeable or disruptable by outside pressures and more autonomous or stable than A. This suggests that T and A are not likely to influence each other equally and that T is less likely to be influenced by changes in A than A is likely to be influenced by changes in T.

After the above had been written we encountered a theoretical analysis by John C. Harsanyi addressed to much the same question considered by our monograph: "What does it mean to ascribe causal priority to one subsystem of the social system over another? It essentially means to assume that, while the main aspects of the first subsystem's development can be explained in terms of internal factors, i.e., in terms of interaction among its own variables, the second subsystem's development has to be explained in essential respects in terms of influences coming from the first subsystem."[3]

Clearly Harsanyi's model parallels the method we have used above for assessing the relative influence of T and A. The "subsystems" to which he refers coincide with and are operationalized by the factors as a whole. The "main aspects" of each subsystem are indicated by the core items. The relative autonomy of each subsystem, that is, the degree to which its development can be explained in terms of the interaction of internal elements or its own variables, is measured by the correlations among the core items. If we know that two subsystems are related, as we do from the high correlation between the two factors A and T, and if we may infer that the one which is relatively more autonomous is "causally prior" to the other, then we may conclude that T influences A more than A influences T or, in Harsanyi's terms, that T is "causally prior" to A. Since we regard this strategy of approaching the problem of causal priority as the more interesting and promising of the several used here, we present a fuller discussion and partial formalization of it in the addendum written by L. Keith Miller.

While in some of the measures used above the differences in the magnitudes of T and A are manifestly unimportant, and it is difficult if not impossible to estimate their relative precedence, there is no question but that the *combination* of these two factors forms the dominant complex within the domain as a whole. Together, they

---

[3] J. C. Harsanyi, "Explanation and Comparative Dynamics in Social Science," *Behavioral Science*, April 1960, p. 144.

comprise the core of what is by far the largest factor that emerges from a "second-order" factor analysis—that is, from a factor analysis of the (oblique) factors, rather than of the original concrete variables.

First, in Table XV below, we indicate the loadings on the largest second-order factor:

TABLE XV ~~

O-factor no.		Loading
5	(Apollonianism)	.89
9	(Technology)	.87
7		.78
8		.65
3		.49
4		.48
11		.44
1		−.44
6		.42
2		.40
10		−.31

As would be expected from the high correlation between T and A, they both emerge as the foremost items on this factor and with scarcely any difference in their loadings. It is also noteworthy that this is a general factor, with all of the first-order factors having an appreciable loading on it, the lowest being .31 and the average loading being above .5. This factor extracts about twice as much variance as the next largest factor and more than a third of the variance in the entire matrix. Moreover, the significance of this relatively large amount of variance—since it is a variance in the factor scores and not in those of the original variables—would not seem to be vitiated in the same way or for the same sampling reasons that the latter would be. This large and general second-order factor suggests that if there is such a thing as a "core complex" common to primitive societies, its nucleus might well be defined in terms of the T and A dimensions.

Having seen that technology and Apollonianism can be represented by a single dimension and are thus in a sense indicative of one entity, the question now presents itself as to how one might conceive of this dimension as a whole. What is it that both A and T might share or have in common? From a limited and quite possibly ethnocentric perspective we are tempted to characterize the positive pole of this dimension as "civilization" or even as "Western civilization," fully cognizant that most of the concrete societies in our sample are in no ordinary sense "Western." Nonetheless, societies commonly viewed as manifesting Western civilization, with their historical roots in Greek culture, do seem in part distinguishable from others by reason of the conjunction of their relatively high Apollonian qualities *and* their relatively great development of technology—a conjunction crucial to this factor.

Beyond this and on a somewhat more analytical level, it may be conjectured that both A and T may commonly contribute to the development of the "capital" of a society—to the surplus of goods and services above that used or consumed in maintaining a desired standard of living. It would seem that there are at least two ways in which this surplus may be increased: through increased productivity and through the development of an ability to defer gratifications, the former being enhanced by T and the latter by A. Moreover, the development of an increased capacity to control impulses and defer gratifications establishes a necessary, if not the sufficient, condition for increasing the rational utilization of resources and, with this, of further growth in capital.

In Conclusion

The posture adopted throughout has been a pragmatic one. We have neither proposed nor pursued any neat hypotheses but, rather, as Claude Bernard put it, have conducted an "experiment to see." In other terminology, we have deliberately sought to devise and place ourselves within a "context of discovery" rather than a "context of proof." In particular, we have sought to explore the utility of factor analysis for coping with a relatively large number of traits in a large number of societies, simultaneously examined.

Our findings are related to two different problems: One set of results provides a provisional identification of certain dimensions of primitive society; in particular, they highlight the potential significance of T and A. Many of the dimensions yielded by the factor analysis are the more interesting for being the less surprising; many of them seem to be readily related to certain traditional anthropological concepts and thus hold promise as tools for the systematic comparison of primitive societies.

Most of these dimensions are by no means new. Our point, however, is not that they comprise substantive discoveries but, rather, in some modest sense, that they entail a methodological "discovery." They do indicate that a purely statistical method can elicit dimensions often corresponding to those of traditional anthropological usage, which had formerly been based largely on qualitative data or derived from informal theoretical conjecture.

Moreover, we certainly do not believe that the dimensions here identified have exhausted the possibilities. Subsequent researches will, beyond doubt, identify other important dimensions and will also lead us to revise our conceptions of those already found. Unless, however, we are confusing expectation with hope, we expect that subsequent replications will produce results consistent with those reported here.

In replications using new *variables*, rather than merely adding to the sample of societies, we would expect the discovery of new factors. We are aware, for example, that recent anthropological developments in kinship analysis and theory would call for either the reclassification of the data we used or the use of additional data and supplementary classification schemes. If, however, these are added to the materials that we employed, then, in addition to newly discovered factors, many of the factors found here should also be discernible in the new results.

Another consequence of replications using new data or new classificatory schemes could well be the addition of new, highly loaded items to clusters or factors already identified, either confirming our prior conceptualization of them or enabling these to be sharpened and revised. Replication along the above lines could, finally, "split" in two a factor that we had already found; we would, however, expect these to have a relatively high correlation with one another. It would seem that these are the most likely though not the only possible results of subsequent replications.

A second major interest of our work involved an attempt to see whether factor analysis and the information it provides had any promise of extricating us from the banalities of functional theory. Going beyond the vague postulate of interdependence, we sought to assess the various magnitudes of the factors and to appraise which are more or less powerful or influential in the entire set of factors extracted.

This concern derived from our dissatisfaction with other basic models of sociological analysis and, particularly, with the functional model which we counterposed to the single-factor and multiple-causation models. In contrast to the functionalist's use of a system composed of unweighted system elements we proposed an alternative that we called the "stratified system model," which makes the following assumptions: (1) sociocultural elements are to be analyzed as part of a system, i.e., in relation to other elements with which they are presumed to interact; (2) the total common variance of systems will differ; (3) the variance in any one element in the system may be only partly accounted for by any other element in it—and, indeed, this is expected to be the usual case; (4) some elements in the system account for more variance in the remaining system elements, while others account for less.

Our effort to pursue the last assumption led us to propose various operationalizations or measures for the notion of "influence." We are soberly aware that we sometimes violated the demanding assumptions entailed by certain of the statistics used; yet we also feel that there was usually a reasonable agreement, a kind of conceptual fit, between these measures and our interests.

All of us are aware that social scientists today often face the choice of using elegant methods on trivial problems or, putting down fastidious inclinations, of confronting basic problems with available methods, even if they have to trim their statistical sails to do so.

We are under no illusion that the problem of assessing the differential influence of different factors in a system has here been definitely solved. We have not found the Northwest Passage. Yet the effort reported on here may have given others a clearer glimpse of where and how to look for it.

Addendum ~~~~

A Methodological Note on Determining
the Causal Priority of Two Variables[1] L. KEITH MILLER

This appendix outlines a tentative solution to the problem of determining which of two variables is causally prior to the other. The
problem of causal priority has been solved in the experimental sciences, in which one variable can be fixed at certain predetermined
values and its effect on other variables investigated. In this case, any
covariation of the two variables indicates an effect of the fixed variable on the other one. The strategy exemplified by the experimental
approach is to make one variable "uninfluenceable" through experimental manipulation and then to investigate its covariation with
other variables.

The problem of causal priority is virtually unsolved in the non-
experimental sciences. For, when data is gathered from a field study,
the effect of one variable on another is always accompanied by the
possibility of a reciprocal influence. In this case, where both variables are simultaneously "influenceable," the covariation between
them is an indicator solely of the amount of influence, but not its
direction. A high degree of covariation might be indicative of the
complete domination of one variable by the other, the mutual influence of each variable on the other, or a degree of asymmetrical influence lying somewhere between the two extremes. Hence, in this

[1] This paper was written for this volume at the suggestion of the senior author.
Gouldner suggested many of the basic ideas and discussed the few new ones at
length with me. I should like to thank Don Bushell for giving the manuscript
a detailed criticism. *L.K.M.*

case the magnitude of influence cannot be disentangled from the direction of influence.

This difficulty is probably one root from which the elaborate organism of "system analysis" has grown within the social and biological sciences. The difficulty is further heightened by the fact that this type of analysis is often accompanied by the tacit assumption that all of the parts of a system exert an equal influence upon one another. As Gouldner and Peterson have persuasively argued in this monograph and Gouldner elsewhere,[2] however, this postulate is not a necessary companion to a system frame of reference, and is, in fact, a hindrance to the proper understanding of systems of social interaction. Instead, one must take as problematic the degree of reciprocal influence. Unfortunately, augmenting this policy directive is dependent upon technical and methodological gear hitherto unavailable to the social sciences.

While Simon[3] has presented a technique for unraveling causal priority, his technique applies only to very restrictive circumstances. *If* the relationships between several variables present a certain type of profile, *then* causal priority can be deduced. If, however, no such profile happens to exist, then causal priority remains unknown.

Recently a paper by Harsanyi[4] has appeared suggesting a key postulate, independently suggested by Gouldner and Peterson in this monograph, which makes the analysis of causal priority possible regardless of the profile of intervariable relationships. It is a general technique depending only on the type of information gathered by the researcher and not on the outcome of the research, as with the method suggested by Simon. Hence, this would appear to provide a methodology by means of which the Gouldner "directive" may be augmented. Unfortunately, however, the Harsanyi paper is confined

---

[2] A. W. Gouldner, "Reciprocity and Autonomy in Functional Theory," in L. Gross, *Symposium on Sociological Theory*, Row, Peterson, Evanston, 1959.

[3] H. A. Simon, "Causation and Influence Relations," in his *Models of Man*, Wiley, New York, 1957.

[4] John C. Harsanyi, "Explanation and Comparative Dynamics in Social Science," *Behavioral Science*, 5, 1960, pp. 136-145.

to a conceptual level and does not, in fact, produce an operational methodology.

This addendum attempts to carry Harsanyi's work the one remaining step to an empirical methodology. Toward this end, it will be divided into two parts. The first part attempts to formalize Harsanyi's argument within a framework amenable to operationalization in terms of correlational statistical procedures. The second part outlines this operationalization and introduces a number of variations on the basic theme.

The Conceptual Basis for the Methodology

Previous approaches to causal analysis have focused on the relationship between two unitary variables. For example, the experimental approach has held one variable constant and allowed the other to vary, while Simon's approach infers the causal priority between two variables from their relationship with other variables. These and other previous approaches have remained on one level of analysis, treating the constituent variables as irreducible. The approach utilized in the present paper relies on multiple levels of analysis. It assumes that variables may be analyzed into systems composed of more elementary variables. In turn, these more elementary variables may themselves be treated as systems. In fact, the elementary particles of modern physics suggest that it may be feasible at any level of analysis to suppose that there is a more elementary level beneath it. However, in the present approach to causality, only two levels of analysis are required. It seeks to infer the causal priority existing *between* two variables from the *internal* structure of each variable analyzed as a system.

In addition to assuming that any variable may be analyzed into more elementary variables, it seems reasonable to assume that systems of variables may be conceptualized as isomorphic to the more usual notion of a system. The most outstanding difference between the two types of systems consists of their "parts." Usually the parts are taken as empiric entities involved in system relations. For example, social systems are defined in terms of roles and their relationships, personality systems as traits and their relations, and so on. There is, however, a fundamental ambiguity which arises from this approach. The same roles may be involved in several social systems. Thus, the President is the President in Cabinet meetings as well as in greeting foreign guests. However, a different *aspect* of the role is manifested in each situation. It seems reasonable to resolve this fundamental ambiguity by singling out relevant aspects of the empiric entity and speaking of this aspect as the "part" in the system. These analytic dimensions of the empiric entities are reasonably conceptualized as variables. Hence, a system may be viewed as the relationship between a set of variables.

The approach here makes these two assumptions which are at variance with usual practice: First, it makes the assumption that variables at any level of analysis can be decomposed into more elementary variables. Secondly, it makes the assumption that these variables form a system, as this concept is usually understood. With these two assumptions we are prepared to discuss the concepts and postulates which have recently been developed by sociologists working with system theory.

It has been all too common in functional analysis to assume that systems are highly interdependent with their variables strongly controlled from within. Parsons' postulate that systems automatically and strongly seek to re-equilibrate themselves is a characteristic example of this. Gouldner[5] has challenged this assumption and suggested that a number of interesting questions and conclusions arise if the interdependence of systems is taken as problematic. The most provocative conclusion in the present context was suggested by both Gouldner and Peterson, in the present monograph, and Harsanyi. They have pointed out that the interdependence of each of two related systems must affect the direction of influence between them. For, if a system is highly interdependent, then by definition the variables are largely controlled by the system. Less interdependent systems, on the other hand, are less subject to internal control and must be controlled by external sources. Thus, if two systems are related, and if they differ in interdependence, the interdependent one exerts

---

[5] *Op. cit.*

more influence on the less interdependent one. These ideas, then, form the basis for a rational model of the influence process between two variables. From the model it is possible to infer the causal priority of the two variables. To do this, a second level of analysis must be added so that the interdependence of the variables-considered-as-systems may be determined. It remains only for us to turn this model into an operational technique. The next section suggests such a technique based on a correlational approach to the model.

Operational Definition of Causal Analysis

This section suggests a number of correlational techniques which might be used to undertake a causal analysis along the lines suggested in the previous section. The basic idea is that the magnitude of the relationship between any two variables may be measured by the correlation coefficient. This in turn suggests the use of multivariate correlational techniques to measure the other concepts involved in the theory. The section will first discuss identifying and measuring systems and later will discuss measuring interdependence.

By definition a system is any set of variables which are related to one another. Consequently, any two variables which are correlated with one another form a system. Further, any set of variables consistently correlated with one another form a common system. The key element of this correlational approach is consistency. We expect the relationships between system members to be consistent, such that if variables A and B are positively related, and A and C are positively related, we would expect B and C also to be positively related. In fact, if A and B are strongly related, and if A and C are strongly related, we expect B and C to be strongly related. Thus, a set of variables should not only exhibit strong correlations between its members but should exhibit consistent relationships. In order to be a system, then, a consistent relationship must run through all of a set of variables. At another level of analysis, however, these same variables may be viewed as a single, higher-level variable. From this perspective, the relationships between the variables may be explained by their common relationship to the higher-level variable.

72   *Notes on*

The principal postulate of factor analysis is that the observed relationships between a set of variables may be explained by an underlying variable which is ordinarily called a "factor."[6] It seems reasonable, then, to define any set of variables which have a factor running
through them as a system (or subsystem). This operational identification actually solves two problems in the proposed model of causal
analysis. On the one hand it provides a technique which may be used
to discover systems—that is, to work with a number of variables and
discover which variables group together into systems. Needless to say,
the *meaning* of these systems must be determined on other grounds.
On the other hand, factor analysis provides a technique whereby the
system may be analyzed on the next higher level of analysis. It provides a method for inferring the value of the system as a variable.
These two implications of defining systems as factors will be taken
up seriatim.

If an investigator is confronted with a large number of variables
whose system properties he does not know, he can conduct a factor
analysis to determine them. Each resulting factor suggests the presence of one system of variables. This provides an empirical technique
for sorting the variables into systems. Unfortunately, this procedure
creates some problems. First of all, each variable will usually be correlated with each factor so that every variable might be included in
every system. By doing this, however, the investigator would be ad-
mitting on equal status variables which were unequally committed
to the system. Thus, it would seem desirable to devise a technique
whereby variables are sorted into mutually exclusive systems with
membership limited to variables strongly related to the system.[7] We
need, then, a criterion whereby the correlation of a variable with a
factor may be deemed sufficiently strong to admit it to the status of

---

[6] For a general discussion of factor analysis and its interpretation consult the
discussion in any general text, such as B. Fruchter, *Introduction to Factor Analysis*, Van Nostrand, Princeton, 1954.

[7] Cluster analysis is designed explicitly for just this purpose. Unfortunately,
however, it can be used only when all of the intercorrelations are positive, an
unusual case in sociology or anthropology. See, for example, K. J. Holzinger and
H. H. Harman, *Factor Analysis*, University of Chicago Press, Chicago, 1951, ch. 11.

"system-member." The simplest criterion is also the most arbitrary: select any correlation between zero and one; below that level exclude the variable, above that level include the variable. Another criterion is the significance test. If a variable is significantly related to the factor by the t-test,[8] then it would be included; if not, it would be excluded.

$$t = \frac{r\sqrt{n-2}}{\sqrt{1-r^2}}$$

A more general approach to this problem is offered by various attempts to create what is called "simple structure" in the factors. Simple structure refers to a pattern of correlations between variables and factors such that each variable appears highly loaded on only one factor. When simple structure exists, or is approximated, the problem of sorting variables into mutually exhaustive systems is considerably simpler.

Simple structure may exist after an initial extraction of factors. If it doesn't, then "rotations" of the initial factors may be undertaken. Such rotations are carried out by altering the initial correlations between factors and variables in a systematic and consistent fashion. There are three widely used methods for rotating factors according to an abstract mathematical criterion. Two of these, the Varimax and Quartimax rotations, maintain the uncorrelated nature of the factors. The other one, the Oblimax, allows the factors to change to correlated factors.[9] All of these rotations were utilized by Gouldner and Peterson in the present monograph.

Since the type of analysis which we are discussing assumes that systems (and therefore factors) are correlated, it seems reasonable to utilize the Oblimax rotation for the initial identification of systems. This, combined with the statistical criterion recommended above,

---

[8] R. Fisher, *Statistical Methods for Research Workers* (12th ed.), Hafner, New York, 1954, p. 193.

[9] D. R. Saunders and C. Pinska, "Analytic Rotation to Simple Structure: Extension to an Oblique Solution," *Research Bulletin*, Princeton Educational Testing Service, 1954.

should provide reasonably clear identification of systems. As this discussion has suggested, factor analysis may provide a method whereby systems of variables may be discovered. If the systems are known *a priori* to the investigator, a situation seldom met in the social sciences, then this product of factor analysis is not required for a causal analysis. It should be noted, however, that the outlines of a system of variables are often known well enough so that the investigator can select variables *a priori* with a good probability that many of them will be members of the system. A factor analysis then clarifies the boundaries of the system. This case is probably the most usual. Factor analysis also solves a second problem in the proposed model of causal analysis by providing a measure of the "system-as-a-whole." Since the relationship between two variables (also to be analyzed as systems) must be determined, the factors must be measured. Consistent with a previous suggestion, the strength of the relationship between the two variables may be measured by the strength of the correlation between the factors. If the factors are based on the initial factor extraction it is impossible for the factors to be correlated, since uncorrelated factors always result by definition. If, however, the initial factors are subjected to an oblique rotation, then the correlation between the resulting factors measures the correlation between the systems. It is important to note that this leads to several difficulties. First of all, it tends to bias the correlation between systems to be higher than it would be. This occurs because the systems share members. Thus, their correlation reflects not only the relationship between them but also the fact that their membership overlaps.

Another procedure is available which minimizes this problem. After the oblique rotation and statistical tests have been used to identify the membership of variables in different systems, each system might be refactored separately. Thus a factor analysis might first be undertaken on all of those variables which have been included in or highly loaded on one system, and then another factor analysis undertaken on all of the variables in the other system. The primary factor resulting from each of these refactorizations might then be used to measure the system as a whole. This would lead to considerably different and more purified factors because the overlapping variables have been eliminated, as have other assorted variables which are not members of any system. In this case, even though the systems were originally derived from orthogonal factors, the refactorization would lead to factors which in general may be correlated. After the refactorization, a correlation analysis between the factors would be undertaken in order to determine the extent and magnitude of the relation between them.[10]

In summary, this section has discussed the definition of systems in terms of correlation and factor analysis. The first problem in a causal analysis is to determine the boundaries and membership of the systems in question. This may be done by means of rotation to oblique simple structure. The second problem in this model of causal analysis is to determine the correlation between two systems. This may be done in two ways. Either the correlation between the factors may be utilized to estimate the correlation between the systems, or the variables in each system may be subjected to a separate refactorization and the correlation between the resulting factors may be determined. Having devised procedures for identifying factors and determining their correlation, it remains now to measure the interdependence of the systems. The next section is concerned with this problem.

Interdependence of Systems or Subsystems

The simplest method for estimating the interdependence of a set of variables is to investigate their intercorrelations. If they are highly intercorrelated, then we would assume that they

---

[10] This would require obtaining individual factor scores for each member of the sample. If a principal components factor analysis is used to extract the factors, then individual factor scores may be derived straightforwardly. If a principal axes factor analysis is used, then a multiple regression technique may be used to estimate individual factor scores. (The difference between principal components and principal axes is that unity is entered in the diagonals in the former and communalities in the latter. The use of the latter seems more justified in this case since a general factor is assumed.) Both methods of estimating individual factor scores are discussed in Godfrey Thompson, *The Factorial Analysis of Human Ability*, Houghton Mifflin, 1946, one of the most readable books on statistics. See particularly chs. 5 and 7.

are highly interdependent. Unfortunately, this simple dictum does not unambiguously point to a single technique whereby the investigator may decide the magnitude of the intercorrelations between the variables. Should the correlations be added; should they be squared first; should their overlap be eliminated; or should their consistency be considered? This section suggests a number of approaches to this problem and points out some of the limitations of each. The simplest technique for determining the magnitude of intercorrelations between the members of a system is to sum the correlations and obtain their mean. The larger the mean, the greater the interdependence. The principal drawback of doing this is that correlations are not on an equal-interval scale. Consequently, the average of a set of correlations is not a very meaningful measure. A more appropriate measure may be obtained by squaring the correlations, thereby transforming them to an equal-interval scale based on variances. Summing these values and obtaining the mean would appear to present us with a simple, and therefore attractive, measure of interdependence.

There are a number of questions which can be raised at this point considering the validity of this operation. First of all, it should be clear that some, perhaps much, of the correlation between two variables in a system is a result of their mutual relationship with other variables in the system. It might be possible to argue, therefore, that the correlations will reflect more determination of one variable by the other than really exists. That is, it is a spurious correlation, and should be eliminated by partial correlation. However, the very essence of "systemness" is this network of reverberating relationships between variables. Consequently, the more of this "spuriousness" there is, the more interdependence exists. To remove it would be to remove much of what we seek to measure.

Another possibility is that part of the correlation between the members of the system reflects extra-system relationships (between them). This is pointed up by the type of inconsistencies which were discussed in connection with the factor-analytic definition of "system." These inconsistencies are excluded from the operational measurement of the system (factor) and, hence, perhaps should not be included in the measurement of interdependence. This could readily be accomplished by virtue of the fact that the amount of correlation between two variables predictable from their common system membership may be estimated by the crossproduct of the correlations with the factor. This provides a measure of the correlation which would be consistent with the other correlations. Therefore, an index of the squares of the consistent correlations summed and the mean obtained from this might be formed. Both this index and the simpler one have much to recommend them. They are both simple and quite direct measures of the interdependence of a system of variables.

Summary

The methodology suggested here is an attempt to apply some recent developments in system analysis to the problem of determining the causal priority of two variables. In order to do this, a departure from previous causal analysis was introduced by analyzing the two variables in question into systems composed of more elementary variables. The homology between systems of this type and the usual conceptualization of systems was pointed out. This homology allows the application of developments by both Gouldner and Harsanyi in system analysis.

The basic advance made by both, and the central postulate of this paper, is that the more internally interdependent of two related systems exerts causal priority over the other.

The conceptual model requires four things: First, that the strength of the relationship between two variables be measured. This is done by means of simple correlation coefficients. Secondly, that the membership of a variable in a system be determined; that is, that the identities of the systems be determined. This is done preferably by a principal axis factor analysis rotated to oblique simple structure. Membership in a system requires that a variable be "significantly" related to the factor. Thirdly, that the system-as-a-whole be treated as a variable and measured so that the correlation between the two systems may be determined. Two approaches to this problem were suggested. Either take the correlation between the oblique factors for this purpose, or conduct a separate factor analysis for each system and correlate the factors. Fourthly, that the interdependence of each system be determined. This may be done by finding the average magnitude of the correlations between the members of the same system.

The causal priority of two related systems may be inferred from the fourth step; the system with the largest average *internal* correlations is assumed to be causally prior to the system with the smallest average internal correlations. Further, the degree of priority is proportional to the difference in these average correlations.

APPENDIX A ~~ *List of Societies Included in Sample*

1. Abipone	25. Eskimo-Polar	49. Munda
2. Ainu	26. Euahlayi	50. Navaho
3. Akamba	27. Fan	51. Norsemen
4. Albanians	28. Haida	52. Omaha
5. Andamanese	29. Hebrew	53. Palaung
6. Araucanians	30. Hopi	54. Pomo
7. Arawak	31. Hottentot	55. Rwala
8. Arunta	32. Iban	56. Samoans
9. Ashanti	33. Inca	57. Semang
10. Aztec	34. Iroquois	58. Sema Naga
11. Bakongo	35. Jivaro	59. Seri
12. Banks Islanders	36. Xosa	60. Shilluk
13. Berber	37. Kazak	61. Tasmanians
14. Bontoc Igorot	38. Kiwai	62. Toda
15. Bushmen	39. Kutenai	63. Trobrianders
16. Chin	40. Kwakiutl	64. Tuareg
17. Chippewa	41. Lango	65. Vai
18. Chukchi	42. Lapp	66. Vedda
19. Creek	43. Lengua	67. Witoto
20. Crow	44. Mafulu	68. Yahgans
21. Dahomeans	45. Maori	69. Yakut
22. Dieri	46. Mangbetu	70. Yuchi
23. Eskimo-Lab.	47. Menomini	71. Yukaghir
24. Eskimo-Pt. B.	48. Mongols	

APPENDIX B ～ Traits Included in Factor Analysis

Simmons' No.	Our No.	Content	Scoring of Blanks
1	1	Permanency of residence	2
2	2	Group life in contrast to atomism	1
3	3	Durability of dwellings	2
4	4	Communal houses	4
5	5	Separate men's houses	4
6	6	Collection	3
7	7	Hunting	2
8	8	Fishing	2
9	9	Herding	3
10	10	Agriculture	2
11	11	Use of grain for food	2
12	12	Constancy of food supply	2
13	13	Domesticated animals other than herded	3
14	14	Mining and smelting of metals	4
15	15	Metals secured from the outside	2
16	16	Pottery	2
17	17	Basketry	1
18	18	Weaving	1
20	19	Uses of bow and arrow	1
23	20	Slavery	3
24	21	Debt-relations	2
26	22	Money, or a standard medium of exchange	2
27	23	Communal ownership of land	2
28	24	Private property in objects other than land	1
29	25	Private property in land	3
31	26	Power vested in the chief	2
33	27	Govt. by restricted council	1
36	28	Prevalence of war	1
38	29	Codified laws	2
40	30	Authority of judges	1
42	31	Matrilocal residence	3
43	32	Patrilocal residence	1
44	33	Matrilineal descent	2

APPENDIX B—*continued*

Simmons' No.	Our No.	Content	Scoring of Blanks
45	34	Patrilineal descent	1
46	35	Matrilineal inheritance	3
47	36	Patrilineal inheritance	1
49	37	Patrilineal succession	1
51	38	Patripotestal family authority	1
56	39	Plutocracy	1
57	40	Exogamy with reference to kin-group	1
61	41	Polygyny	2
62	42	Monogamy	1
64	43	Marriage by choice of authority	1
65	44	Marriage by capture	3
66	45	Marriage by purchase or bride price	1
72	46	Difficulty of divorce for women	2
74	47	Subjection or inferiority of women	2
75	48	Uncleanness of women	2
76	49	Postmarital sex restriction on women	2
81	50	Organized priesthood	3
84	51	Elaboration of ceremonial and ritual	2
85	52	Legendary heroes	1
92	53	Intensity of ghost-fear	1
94	54	Abandonment of the house of the dead	3
96	55	Mortuary sacrifice of property	2
97	56	Elaboration of mortuary ceremonies	2
98	57	Attractiveness of future life	2
	58	Climatic conditions: severe, temperate, warm	
	59	Danger of famine or not	

APPENDIX C ～ *Correlation Matrix for Traits in Appendix B*

(Decimals are assumed before first digit.)

CORRELATIONS (r)

	1	2	3	4	5	6	7	8	9	10	11	12	13	14	15	16
1		540	482	113	352	−427	−244	007	−175	724	461	521	410	282	265	323
2			277	044	347	−259	−175	041	−134	330	189	347	250	188	176	270
3				213	019	−533	−285	−017	−066	381	252	223	181	153	176	143
4					−085	157	047	272	−320	075	−032	056	−038	−117	008	054
5						−057	−136	−042	−130	242	−074	142	262	012	150	070
6							581	341	−372	−459	−338	−234	−388	−381	−233	−253
7								410	−327	−375	−175	−171	−304	−296	−070	−149
8									−422	−151	−287	137	−079	−205	−071	−237
9										−030	290	−232	267	443	243	252
10											593	561	498	324	145	457
11												387	373	444	405	625
12													295	137	138	297
13														417	400	374
14															225	480
15																205

	17	18	19	20	21	22	23	24	25	26	27	28	29	30	31	32
1	089	126	−199	286	199	323	−217	242	376	376	125	355	428	274	−169	133
2	249	176	−075	229	087	260	069	059	179	278	−003	431	151	074	−136	024
3	047	165	−113	361	206	186	−161	−050	393	276	−111	216	254	026	026	028
4	218	−008	093	−071	−047	−088	089	097	064	003	−133	129	−139	−057	162	−188
5	236	004	−217	−155	102	148	−226	195	251	032	036	045	094	135	−190	153
6	166	−092	057	−275	−359	−280	227	028	−401	−272	−034	−183	−456	−176	216	−132
7	000	−125	101	−157	−363	−199	339	−066	−454	−179	−077	−173	−309	−081	329	−228
8	139	195	204	052	−211	−145	108	−124	−089	−050	−033	093	−225	−017	159	−120
9	−008	109	100	178	232	166	−001	−010	−034	165	156	145	305	033	−286	250
10	172	314	−064	288	311	335	−190	231	478	432	158	346	426	219	−198	138
11	202	490	−077	328	331	533	−029	261	227	450	246	407	423	267	−016	037
12	202	371	027	179	223	235	−007	230	282	186	199	293	264	149	007	−011
13	248	266	−007	309	259	271	−232	059	308	308	134	400	347	022	−260	153
14	160	201	−007	470	242	306	−197	−094	318	314	210	425	557	205	−348	293

APPENDIX C *(continued)*

CORRELATIONS (r) —cont.

	17	18	19	20	21	22	23	24	25	26	27	28	29	30	31	32
15	−049	232	−204	350	350	342	−028	053	058	232	085	252	284	124	−114	066
16	391	386	−037	191	214	381	052	053	194	241	−001	502	281	164	048	−065
17		375	139	118	−029	253	033	184	161	219	064	386	−006	033	−001	−036
18			103	229	164	304	059	123	150	335	213	345	224	169	−037	−069
19				−086	063	014	081	025	046	−057	213	−022	−006	−034	134	−135
20					270	234	−064	079	280	504	083	533	400	099	−242	173
21						545	−135	388	286	236	186	125	231	108	−242	256
22							−126	369	424	237	192	315	267	290	−135	163
23								−060	−592	012	−014	−058	−291	−087	002	−115
24									308	140	263	087	110	171	−091	175
25										106	014	214	300	203	−094	188
26											462	418	408	357	−328	243
27												004	312	421	−303	261
28													291	191	−111	009
29														480	−243	201
30															−048	016
31																−813

	33	34	35	36	37	38	39	40	41	42	43	44	45	46
1	−053	−057	078	−008	−057	−110	170	095	039	−163	−105	−074	−088	−006
2	−066	−048	052	−005	−097	−061	−046	103	−076	−064	084	−150	071	128
3	−114	069	135	055	−051	036	208	−128	−268	224	190	−028	−079	013
4	−028	−105	090	−197	−179	−116	−175	061	−372	310	088	013	−070	−176
5	−007	−210	030	−061	−161	−201	−035	171	067	−188	004	−168	221	−007
6	385	−218	020	−179	−131	−016	−306	111	−117	079	−038	247	001	−092
7	278	028	000	063	052	037	−276	079	−067	111	023	149	−160	−122
8	200	−099	099	−122	−267	−103	−173	−019	−035	043	178	−025	−067	−096
9	−299	247	−348	254	236	263	342	−026	186	−165	099	−081	422	144
10	−073	−059	102	−045	014	−138	158	070	161	−282	−137	−100	−113	058
11	035	109	008	130	193	123	416	113	045	−098	−128	−093	−012	111
12	065	−078	292	−070	−157	−179	127	140	138	−124	−016	−195	−178	085
13	−022	092	005	047	−054	013	194	−025	243	−251	046	−033	217	059
14	−260	142	−123	114	082	130	371	022	199	−282	084	045	300	361
15	025	047	074	099	−033	032	076	111	−092	−097	−087	−103	104	078
16	025	−001	069	−063	−052	−131	257	172	062	−147	053	158	049	099
17	097	−054	037	−030	−075	−009	073	214	−184	103	403	065	260	189

APPENDIX C *(continued)*

CORRELATIONS *(r)* —cont.

	33	34	35	36	37	38	39	40	41	42	43	44	45	46
18	157	−113	157	−056	−087	031	259	074	021	−112	115	−067	062	068
19	048	−068	−005	−123	−065	−022	−135	033	047	072	315	−026	102	−043
20	−046	076	099	−037	−036	035	404	066	059	−148	165	054	151	218
21	−125	−005	−044	−012	009	098	281	−086	211	−233	−157	−185	150	088
22	093	−024	015	061	048	002	474	232	098	−117	−099	−030	216	179
23	054	−010	−050	−059	−067	−044	−107	045	021	−004	−154	004	−019	−146
24	099	−027	024	042	115	039	227	107	019	−115	−129	−192	−021	−038
25	−030	−076	171	010	−092	−104	252	122	−013	−063	081	−095	014	164
26	−056	−046	−036	−042	−061	−097	245	016	149	−149	085	−079	028	073
27	−028	−059	−155	123	065	145	212	101	199	−100	−026	−148	051	133
28	003	005	072	−121	−041	−098	279	220	199	−144	220	170	182	073
29	−152	040	−029	030	102	−019	282	−026	145	−188	136	−066	106	223
30	110	−196	101	075	034	−147	284	252	126	−126	−056	−135	−037	015
31	463	−193	398	−172	−147	−227	−174	−056	−425	435	201	−024	−292	−150
32	−383	341	−417	309	258	384	227	−011	407	−285	−192	094	321	191
33		−594	592	−424	−360	−387	007	165	−080	038	087	074	−193	−251
34			−592	656	588	662	075	−296	071	210	015	251	148	261
35				−560	−491	−635	069	114	−174	−042	095	−145	−334	−156
36					701	651	178	−192	114	161	026	027	192	171
37						575	078	−082	242	116	123	197	225	136
38							144	−239	040	156	−052	200	221	274
39								047	267	−160	030	−026	241	115
40									027	−152	−030	−092	136	−157
41										−550	−022	021	262	056
42											267	252	−115	−118
43												056	214	077
44													114	156
45														212

APPENDIX C (continued)

CORRELATIONS (r) —cont.

	47	48	49	50	51	52	53	54	55	56	57	58	59
1	−025	135	−006	234	119	−001	−127	−525	−060	212	150	−251	−328
2	056	076	073	167	018	−067	−130	−350	049	159	002	−256	−246
3	−111	000	096	252	180	001	−055	−407	073	184	248	169	−338
4	−383	074	255	047	−003	−229	248	077	134	−058	−030	−203	−124
5	−104	121	189	−091	014	040	035	−066	089	−160	−055	−357	−115
6	−149	022	108	−387	−265	−095	035	550	065	−215	−181	−214	200
7	−072	164	206	−274	−114	−033	066	455	076	−157	096	066	041
8	−233	099	112	−240	−188	033	−025	064	047	−127	−198	020	037
9	214	015	−028	365	141	226	−053	001	−183	−021	038	252	078
10	−063	047	171	241	088	−114	−019	−468	−109	267	058	−396	−133
11	160	137	190	421	238	085	−023	−204	−196	231	364	−140	−133
12	−078	−064	071	145	126	−054	−034	−281	−008	344	149	−341	−120
13	−018	023	−040	221	−109	044	−021	−281	−073	155	−083	−158	−129
14	166	134	108	365	−005	048	015	−208	−037	151	135	−088	−060
15	005	025	071	156	349	122	058	−122	−054	327	339	−013	002
16	−015	−033	193	213	178	−104	−007	−064	−088	045	183	−350	−109
17	−116	098	304	003	−021	−037	140	089	−011	−064	−200	−305	−099
18	077	001	227	181	074	137	184	−116	−039	137	049	−114	−033
19	−073	085	−037	115	−001	349	250	132	−112	−015	−155	161	009
20	−048	090	100	254	090	034	002	−356	051	114	195	068	−105
21	092	−053	033	234	328	070	103	−203	−036	296	311	−035	−037
22	131	169	073	271	245	219	−039	−248	−117	083	183	−046	−125
23	028	017	062	093	−005	−025	−054	285	134	−012	123	−202	−019
24	−044	054	137	172	287	057	167	−078	−071	−015	148	−126	−214
25	−106	085	144	082	120	057	028	−428	−148	125	−087	−011	−138
26	031	077	190	405	321	141	−100	−359	−003	225	211	−148	−218
27	014	−016	050	231	200	491	081	−016	−137	041	142	−126	007
28	002	222	111	249	065	100	−172	−326	025	−106	−082	−142	−123
29	093	093	−095	473	334	141	178	−320	001	199	257	139	−029
30	−046	212	096	198	343	217	130	−140	−206	−031	079	016	040
31	−236	036	058	−179	−032	−221	098	216	−163	−165	118	127	047
32	253	−022	−085	137	115	199	−130	−183	−055	056	−053	013	−163
33	−342	070	149	−256	−047	034	−004	211	036	060	055	−022	060
34	441	069	−221	165	−046	−069	−053	−025	−146	−080	−028	255	−065
35	−410	−182	135	−099	044	−107	052	−077	073	130	173	−082	−075
36	576	175	−084	085	009	088	−027	−046	−314	−003	012	232	030
37	510	233	−152	025	013	102	021	044	−193	−105	−025	212	−050
38	414	102	−210	098	−154	095	019	152	−211	−102	−094	245	086

APPENDIX C *(continued)*

CORRELATIONS (r) —cont.

	47	48	49	50	51	52	53	54	55	56	57	58	59
39	178	140	−119	388	075	276	−057	−257	−201	−025	128	172	−082
40	−261	091	143	−246	014	046	164	111	183	−009	−080	−135	−100
41	214	073	−217	142	−014	353	−167	−062	−039	095	−167	−109	111
42	008	151	107	−026	016	−106	026	107	−021	−166	026	245	−113
43	−008	165	109	086	081	205	107	069	−047	029	−118	235	045
44	141	207	−116	−127	−163	−013	−124	144	014	−199	−155	007	−077
45	162	123	−061	230	012	225	137	028	089	−066	−238	−075	−033
46	246	−110	144	181	026	036	059	036	−191	006	−073	−170	116
47		213	−181	288	−003	174	−145	−166	−189	064	055	147	060
48			121	182	−021	276	012	025	−079	011	−112	086	062
49				−036	−001	−099	176	202	035	079	075	−263	−028
50					397	215	−014	−234	−060	192	223	−036	017
51						175	117	−210	015	276	276	033	032
52							038	−021	−121	−057	026	159	−017
53								214	084	063	066	040	−120
54									157	016	003	−117	337
55										309	124	−119	−099
56											319	−157	071
57												066	−243
58													−100

APPENDIX D ～ *The Varimax Factor Matrix*

(Decimals are assumed after the first digit in factor loadings and after the second digit in h².)

h²	Trait No.	1(T)	2(L)	3(SD)	4	5	6	7(NS)	8	9	10
+0073	1	+0296	−0009	−0037	+0665	−0088	+0070	+0173	+0377	+0108	+0007
+0049	2	0276	+0009	−0015	+0468	−0221	+0194	+0157	+0202	−0198	−0081
+0063	3	+0208	+0068	+0292	+0291	+0157	+0344	+0238	+0452	−0058	−0083
+0045	4	−0067	−0118	+0402	+0103	−0258	+0401	−0040	−0056	+0053	−0158
+0053	5	−0092	−0092	−0222	+0202	−0557	+0069	+0062	+0309	+0111	+0002
+0071	6	−0265	−0163	+0046	−0075	−0188	−0014	−0328	−0669	+0099	−0093
+0061	7	−0118	−0012	+0219	−0009	−0027	+0009	−0132	−0714	+0072	−0131
+0050	8	−0100	−0248	+0120	+0219	−0023	+0202	−0189	−0272	−0037	−0461
+0075	9	+0380	+0320	−0280	−0560	+0056	−0156	+0249	+0112	−0088	+0037
+0072	10	+0442	−0050	−0089	+0507	−0220	−0074	+0076	+0401	+0112	+0154
+0081	11	+0705	+0166	+0086	+0232	−0007	−0209	+0285	+0024	+0295	+0124
+0056	12	+0324	−0180	−0032	+0591	−0120	−0050	+0079	+0138	+0150	+0069
+0052	13	+0551	+0024	−0218	+0117	−0135	+0138	−0046	+0336	−0051	+0031
+0065	14	+0654	+0204	−0240	−0078	−0085	−0107	+0124	+0226	−0179	−0043
+0043	15	+0375	+0033	+0007	+0015	−0008	+0164	+0462	+0001	+0116	+0171
+0068	16	+0760	−0047	+0058	+0073	−0224	−0123	−0009	+0050	+0057	+0154
+0062	17	+0374	−0008	+0127	+0010	−0562	+0128	−0126	−0004	+0118	−0313
+0044	18	+0546	−0081	+0090	+0178	−0109	−0059	+0119	−0088	+0163	−0174
+0036	19	+0004	−0126	+0047	−0257	−0079	−0127	−0110	−0031	−0028	−0493
+0058	20	+0577	−0006	−0099	+0011	+0223	+0306	+0234	+0145	+0021	−0144
+0050	21	+0254	+0010	−0213	−0135	+0001	+0089	+0324	+0326	+0358	+0167
+0059	22	+0450	+0026	−0093	+0043	−0024	−0139	+0132	+0283	+0501	−0078
+0048	23	+0036	−0021	−0065	+0000	+0033	+0105	+0101	−0661	−0101	+0053
+0057	24	+0023	+0037	−0026	+0068	−0135	+0021	+0193	+0080	+0709	+0032
+0071	25	+0174	−0072	+0033	+0169	−0122	−0059	−0040	+0736	+0264	−0109
+0061	26	+0372	+0011	−0196	+0271	−0076	+0135	+0545	+0005	+0004	−0195
+0052	27	+0023	+0098	−0311	+0131	−0170	−0290	+0367	−0127	+0261	−0252
+0070	28	+0696	−0085	−0118	+0175	+0029	+0238	−0015	+0100	+0022	−0302
+0054	29	+0427	+0062	−0069	+0047	+0058	−0137	+0437	+0338	−0066	−0113
+0052	30	+0099	−0117	−0018	+0157	−0028	−0380	+0403	+0087	+0297	−0263
+0076	31	−0024	−0319	+0741	−0078	+0107	−0233	−0139	−0127	−0001	−0026
+0070	32	−0039	+0448	−0635	+0068	−0020	+0174	+0085	+0138	+0167	+0017
+0063	33	+0086	−0634	+0160	+0113	+0099	−0124	−0112	−0290	+0222	−0091
+0074	34	+0069	+0820	+0044	−0041	+0168	+0125	−0106	+0020	−0040	+0051
+0068	35	+0114	−0741	+0230	+0151	+0162	−0033	+0039	+0051	+0066	+0091
+0073	36	−0064	+0824	+0032	+0055	+0041	−0145	+0096	+0019	+0091	−0042
+0061	37	+0018	+0744	−0018	−0058	+0103	−0063	−0051	−0022	+0182	−0024

APPENDIX D *(continued)*

THE VARIMAX FACTOR MATRIX—cont.

h²	Trait No.	1(T)	2(L)	3(SD)	4	5	6	7(NS)	8	9	10
+0069	38	+0005	+0801	−0031	−0081	+0105	−0001	−0119	−0085	+0091	−0034
+0061	39	+0392	+0113	−0224	−0047	+0352	−0170	+0119	+0209	+0385	−0178
+0040	40	+0128	−0267	−0143	−0054	−0324	+0088	−0072	−0060	+0400	−0048
+0061	41	+0135	+0038	−0763	+0042	+0146	−0133	−0084	−0013	+0062	−0118
+0060	42	−0203	+0212	+0660	+0028	+0086	+0152	−0065	−0025	−0024	−0212
+0055	43	+0155	−0039	+0179	−0189	−0106	+0125	+0041	+0127	−0239	−0592
+0043	44	+0163	+0234	+0023	+0088	+0173	+0118	−0491	−0197	−0062	−0130
+0057	45	+0187	+0281	−0354	−0387	−0238	+0168	−0009	+0102	−0021	−0299
+0038	46	+0238	+0346	−0052	−0013	−0217	−0300	−0015	+0128	−0215	−0025
+0057	47	+0060	+0635	−0117	+0100	+0215	−0259	+0078	−0011	−0118	−0052
+0038	48	+0098	+0183	+0014	+0119	+0018	−0055	−0031	−0065	+0111	−0551
+0044	49	+0186	−0097	+0233	+0030	−0539	−0011	+0146	−0157	+0066	−0069
+0054	50	+0319	+0210	−0091	+0029	+0165	−0129	+0510	+0119	−0148	−0219
+0055	51	−0021	−0059	+0009	−0012	+0023	−0020	+0707	+0101	+0182	−0048
+0059	52	−0018	+0063	−0356	−0041	+0132	−0192	+0171	−0011	+0205	−0578
+0041	53	−0029	−0016	+0317	−0331	−0328	+0059	+0126	+0016	+0233	−0118
+0065	54	−0126	−0007	+0078	−0360	−0297	−0108	−0205	−0594	+0004	+0042
+0047	55	−0065	−0210	−0105	+0009	−0094	+0585	+0048	−0160	−0135	+0110
+0038	56	+0061	−0082	−0143	+0266	−0149	+0115	+0433	+0037	−0132	+0192
+0056	57	+0204	+0001	+0202	+0035	+0174	+0065	+0540	−0164	+0039	−0236
+0061	58	−0147	+0166	+0223	−0361	+0588	+0069	+0081	+0153	+0039	−0236
+0038	59	−0110	−0127	−0148	−0184	−0017	−0431	−0013	−0137	−0263	−0020

Absolute Variance

1	+0524
2	+0517
3	+0355
4	+0291
5	+0258
6	+0207
7	+0343
8	+0399
9	+0230
10	+0258

APPENDIX E ～ The Oblimax Factor Matrix

(Decimals are assumed after first digit.)

PRIMARY FACTOR CORRELATIONS

1	+1000									
2	−0264	+1000								
3	−0236	+0205	+1000							
4	−0135	+0420	+0113	+1000						
5	−0410	+0289	+0357	+0372	+1000					
6	−0113	+0017	+0240	−0131	+0356	+1000				
7	−0243	+0052	+0324	+0116	+0711	+0327	+1000			
8	−0002	−0064	+0222	+0137	+0604	+0262	+0637	+1000		
9	−0484	+0419	+0330	+0501	+0761	+0203	+0595	+0506	+1000	
10	+0054	−0392	−0110	−0586	−0122	−0061	−0022	+0077	−0193	+1000
11	+0163	−0032	+0073	+0045	+0293	+0358	+0468	+0394	+0196	−0267	+1000
	1	*2*	*3*	*4*	*5*	*6*	*7*	*8*	*9*	*10*	*11*

PRIMARY FACTOR PATTERN

	1(SD)	2	3	4	5(NS)	6(L)	7	8	9(T)	10	11
1	−0025	−0331	−0075	+0637	+0141	+0037	+0267	−0084	+0164	+0200	+0281
2	+0095	−0457	+0177	+0253	+0251	−0069	−0129	+0118	+0244	−0217	+0174
3	+0291	+0300	+0063	+0373	+0074	+0124	+0422	+0326	−0248	+0099	−0035
4	+0438	−0132	−0134	+0201	+0054	−0013	−0046	+0365	−0074	−0367	−0354
5	−0161	−0676	−0178	+0064	+0236	−0142	+0402	+0012	−0124	−0399	−0220
6	−0069	−0221	−0098	+0157	−0220	−0021	−0597	+0017	+0034	−0095	−0121
7	+0048	+0058	+0005	+0344	−0126	+0228	−0671	+0067	+0006	+0149	−0227
8	−0152	+0156	+0155	+0747	−0279	−0035	−0031	+0241	−0572	−0011	−0164
9	−0072	+0160	+0037	−1142	+0300	+0021	−0184	−0082	+0597	−0498	−0109
10	−0084	−0393	−0042	+0453	−0206	+0022	+0481	−0141	+0533	+0204	+0058
11	+0190	−0085	−0220	−0003	+0167	+0229	−0164	−0340	+1135	+0177	−0028
12	−0171	−0244	−0019	+0805	−0185	+0013	+0260	−0070	+0237	+0455	+0066
13	−0256	−0086	+0083	−0025	−0537	+0001	+0364	+0284	+0512	−0207	−0067
14	−0158	−0050	+0250	−0426	−0166	+0064	+0088	−0032	+0762	−0308	−0097
15	+0009	+0112	−0115	−0145	+0384	+0054	−0267	+0340	+0301	+0094	−0216
16	+0267	−0349	−0051	−0351	−0222	−0110	−0150	−0183	+1493	−0254	−0058
17	+0232	−0458	−0138	−0141	−0129	+0014	+0082	+0015	+0693	−0831	−0549
18	+0026	+0009	−0032	+0248	−0072	+0054	−0039	−0080	+0615	−0007	−0271
19	−0025	+0223	+0135	−0054	−0069	−0108	+0322	−0196	−0234	−0378	−0414
20	−0195	+0453	+0012	−0066	−0086	−0028	−0062	+0501	+0206	−0112	−0013
21	−0243	+0197	−0398	−0286	+0184	−0011	+0353	+0221	+0062	−0013	−0210
22	−0017	+0019	−0506	−0159	+0142	+0006	+0335	−0334	+0620	−0176	−0042

APPENDIX E *(continued)*

	1(SD)	2	3	4	5(NS)	6(L)	7	8	9(T)	10	11
23	−0054	−0149	+0059	−0149	+0343	−0064	−1217	+0230	+0297	−0025	+0027
24	−0055	−0053	−0773	+0086	+0353	+0162	+0205	−0111	+0052	−0025	−0220
25	+0030	+0027	−0223	+0262	−0268	−0016	+1244	−0238	−0058	−0063	−0216
26	−0161	−0145	+0017	+0022	+0836	−0094	−0484	+0145	+0082	−0180	+0057
27	−0421	−0164	−0136	+0213	+0678	+0148	−0088	−0384	−0264	−0046	−0187
28	−0074	+0015	−0031	−0093	−0157	−0196	−0221	+0218	+0726	−0498	+0203
29	+0005	+0145	+0160	−0145	+0461	−0039	+0229	−0177	+0194	−0001	−0095
30	+0078	−0084	−0213	+0083	+0936	−0162	+0061	−0705	+0045	+0048	−0012
31	+0898	+0206	+0058	+0092	−0029	−0198	+0113	−0488	+0453	+0234	−0204
32	−0817	−0067	−0215	+0011	−0057	+0413	+0044	+0343	−0499	−0117	+0170
33	+0034	+0151	−0126	+0413	−0112	−0485	−0119	−0150	+0188	+0334	+0035
34	+0014	+0210	+0021	−0041	−0444	+0899	−0012	+0140	+0054	−0012	+0005
35	+0173	+0225	+0003	+0361	−0037	−0660	+0186	+0004	+0088	+0477	+0079
36	+0029	+0029	−0051	+0099	+0079	+0926	+0075	−0304	−0115	+0087	−0106
37	−0050	+0142	−0178	−0033	−0202	+0838	+0047	−0159	+0050	−0010	−0060
38	−0129	+0192	−0067	+0028	−0407	+0934	+0025	−0012	−0041	+0000	−0114
39	−0213	+0396	−0365	−0211	+0136	+0024	+0143	−0331	+0326	−0025	+0297
40	−0156	−0271	−0470	−0135	−0019	−0247	+0017	+0094	+0329	−0401	−0234
41	−0994	+0044	+0011	+0046	−0266	−0049	−0044	+0015	−0214	+0043	+0425
42	+0777	+0204	−0013	+0192	+0120	+0322	+0049	−0101	−0158	−0099	−0193
43	+0194	+0235	+0311	−0127	+0103	−0093	+0270	+0073	−0231	−0629	−0469
44	−0046	+0088	+0059	+0171	−0824	+0294	−0219	+0089	+0367	−0119	+0315
45	−0264	−0100	−0080	−0775	+0071	+0052	−0048	+0220	+0130	−0978	−0237
46	+0016	−0242	+0325	−0114	−0193	+0334	+0271	−0364	+0421	−0107	−0242
47	−0039	+0000	+0163	−0055	+0179	+0563	−0231	−0444	+0122	+0117	+0349
48	+0029	+0021	−0068	+0147	+0251	+0166	−0099	−0340	−0034	−0395	+0053
49	+0278	−0412	−0014	+0043	+0198	+0030	−0038	−0018	+0425	−0287	−0701
50	+0110	+0071	+0169	−0383	+0933	−0034	−0385	−0287	+0201	−0189	+0214
51	+0147	+0059	−0221	−0253	+1313	−0186	−0238	−0113	−0281	−0006	−0094
52	−0507	+0273	−0094	+0103	+0468	+0020	+0090	−0330	−0604	−0192	+0017
53	+0306	+0111	−0218	−0177	+0108	+0135	+0413	+0085	−0071	−0313	−0915
54	+0005	−0152	+0029	−0225	−0280	+0127	−0415	+0043	+0260	−0156	−0529
55	−0256	+0009	+0039	+0063	−0129	−0186	−0388	+0980	−0399	−0134	−0082
56	−0261	−0156	+0202	+0335	+0360	−0016	−0094	+0357	−0321	+0355	−0149
57	+0203	+0261	−0146	−0011	+0570	+0095	−0454	+0203	+0204	+0504	−0125
58	+0160	+0962	−0024	−0160	+0061	+0163	+0303	+0044	−0656	+0128	−0009
59	−0130	−0075	+0375	−0188	+0106	−0214	−0040	−0436	−0014	+0131	−0001

APPENDIX F ～ *The Centroid Matrix*

CENTROID FACTORS

$1-h^2$		1	2	3	4	5	6	7
+0.205	1	+0.572	—0.432	—0.114	+0.307	—0.115	—0.102	—0.167
+0.404	2	+0.394	—0.332	+0.142	+0.269	—0.280	+0.092	—0.088
+0.317	3	+0.353	—0.385	+0.232	+0.337	+0.258	+0.131	—0.182
+0.407	4	—0.200	—0.404	+0.320	+0.125	—0.094	—0.137	+0.168
+0.335	5	+0.262	—0.252	—0.285	+0.184	—0.343	—0.103	+0.247
+0.208	6	—0.603	+0.100	+0.063	—0.256	—0.354	—0.269	+0.211
+0.266	7	—0.468	+0.091	+0.289	—0.266	—0.162	—0.249	+0.168
+0.329	8	—0.307	—0.184	+0.171	—0.113	—0.343	—0.116	—0.169
+0.209	9	+0.432	+0.430	+0.150	—0.297	+0.193	+0.296	+0.081
+0.168	10	+0.607	—0.413	—0.146	+0.225	—0.159	—0.121	—0.147
+0.152	11	+0.669	—0.206	+0.189	—0.189	+0.144	—0.215	—0.037
+0.325	12	+0.386	—0.454	—0.142	+0.103	—0.197	—0.158	—0.147
+0.344	13	+0.536	—0.171	+0.084	+0.104	—0.217	+0.148	—0.152
+0.220	14	+0.635	+0.095	+0.218	—0.104	—0.104	—0.121	+0.198
+0.443	15	+0.414	—0.225	+0.152	—0.126	+0.172	+0.196	+0.242
+0.211	16	+0.462	—0.293	+0.251	—0.155	—0.136	—0.083	—0.101
+0.254	17	+0.222	—0.267	+0.364	—0.130	—0.408	—0.291	+0.094
+0.400	18	+0.364	—0.284	+0.244	—0.286	—0.130	—0.161	—0.109
+0.328	19	—0.121	+0.074	+0.130	—0.350	—0.132	—0.104	—0.195
+0.236	20	+0.491	—0.175	+0.266	—0.153	+0.056	+0.311	—0.147
+0.359	21	+0.507	—0.128	—0.195	—0.120	+0.240	+0.113	+0.216
+0.309	22	+0.592	—0.167	—0.104	—0.242	+0.126	—0.258	—0.052
+0.353	23	—0.234	+0.112	+0.213	—0.243	—0.196	+0.139	+0.235
+0.361	24	+0.311	—0.183	—0.229	—0.157	+0.169	—0.390	+0.350
+0.221	25	+0.467	—0.336	—0.232	+0.185	+0.105	—0.217	—0.250
+0.278	26	+0.575	—0.207	+0.109	—0.176	—0.132	+0.208	+0.084
+0.321	27	+0.377	+0.135	—0.207	—0.346	—0.142	—0.190	+0.163
+0.202	28	+0.491	—0.258	+0.303	—0.168	—0.268	+0.110	—0.293
+0.352	29	+0.612	—0.109	+0.063	—0.133	+0.162	+0.184	—0.175
+0.333	30	+0.355	—0.154	—0.207	—0.378	+0.115	—0.234	—0.074

APPENDIX F *(continued)*

CENTROID FACTORS—cont.

	8	9	10	11	12	13	14	15
1	−0.222	−0.068	−0.032	−0.096	+0.123	−0.081	−0.104	−0.161
2	−0.114	−0.082	−0.140	−0.232	−0.134	+0.117	+0.115	+0.073
3	−0.151	+0.180	−0.142	+0.114	+0.082	−0.049	−0.117	+0.124
4	−0.064	+0.222	−0.141	−0.134	+0.141	−0.269	−0.167	+0.066
5	+0.212	+0.092	−0.210	−0.123	−0.135	+0.273	+0.086	−0.125
6	−0.136	−0.035	+0.095	−0.067	+0.088	+0.142	+0.180	+0.118
7	−0.308	−0.125	+0.061	+0.151	+0.084	+0.172	−0.081	−0.236
8	−0.305	+0.218	−0.170	+0.270	+0.097	−0.097	+0.232	−0.161
9	+0.355	−0.029	+0.095	−0.105	−0.075	−0.106	+0.084	−0.083
10	+0.049	−0.167	+0.127	+0.067	+0.073	−0.254	−0.165	−0.110
11	−0.087	−0.309	+0.285	−0.042	−0.062	−0.120	−0.110	−0.033
12	−0.197	−0.190	+0.105	+0.213	−0.187	−0.174	+0.071	+0.041
13	+0.188	+0.082	+0.230	+0.138	−0.163	−0.165	+0.166	−0.184
14	+0.258	−0.112	+0.129	+0.096	+0.281	+0.098	−0.143	+0.098
15	−0.110	−0.118	+0.111	+0.132	−0.142	+0.195	+0.124	−0.199
16	+0.241	−0.253	+0.373	−0.231	−0.052	−0.124	−0.172	−0.074
17	+0.240	+0.166	−0.042	−0.158	−0.111	−0.049	+0.264	+0.140
18	−0.085	−0.096	+0.115	+0.185	−0.161	−0.218	+0.188	+0.130
19	+0.168	+0.221	−0.247	+0.226	−0.203	−0.398	−0.208	+0.124
20	−0.151	+0.201	+0.180	+0.168	+0.308	+0.151	+0.156	+0.108
21	+0.100	+0.162	+0.154	+0.149	−0.192	−0.122	−0.132	+0.218
22	+0.061	+0.139	+0.181	−0.136	−0.133	+0.130	−0.104	+0.196
23	−0.341	−0.241	+0.139	−0.249	−0.157	−0.225	−0.130	+0.120
24	−0.118	+0.200	+0.095	−0.077	−0.093	−0.149	+0.986	+0.135
25	+0.282	+0.286	−0.085	+0.164	+0.102	+0.115	−0.056	+0.134
26	−0.297	−0.078	−0.174	−0.091	+0.259	−0.153	+0.112	+0.038
27	−0.189	−0.117	−0.253	+0.201	+0.161	−0.233	+0.145	+0.132
28	−0.103	+0.208	+0.211	−0.250	+0.069	+0.053	+0.091	−0.150
29	+0.060	−0.109	−0.153	+0.156	+0.216	−0.052	−0.141	−0.130
30	−0.120	−0.123	−0.288	−0.096	+0.274	+0.089	−0.090	−0.212

APPENDIX F (continued)

CENTROID FACTORS—cont.

1-h²		1	2	3	4	5	6	7
+0.173	31	−0.491	−0.354	+0.251	−0.163	+0.325	−0.290	−0.260
+0.217	32	+0.475	+0.433	−0.249	+0.187	−0.167	+0.099	+0.257
+0.256	33	−0.324	−0.436	−0.128	−0.434	−0.086	−0.147	−0.197
+0.206	34	+0.239	+0.551	+0.380	+0.390	+0.197	−0.115	+0.069
+0.239	35	−0.215	−0.656	−0.198	−0.226	+0.100	+0.102	−0.268
+0.171	36	+0.331	+0.553	+0.205	+0.267	+0.220	−0.313	+0.138
+0.265	37	+0.270	+0.551	+0.207	+0.182	+0.196	−0.295	+0.120
+0.231	38	+0.209	+0.628	+0.287	+0.230	+0.134	−0.250	+0.122
+0.306	39	+0.523	+0.127	−0.114	−0.310	+0.239	−0.082	−0.243
+0.438	40	+0.072	−0.255	−0.143	−0.272	−0.250	−0.188	+0.232
+0.230	41	+0.322	+0.391	−0.386	−0.196	−0.341	+0.165	−0.144
+0.326	42	−0.291	−0.078	+0.450	+0.216	+0.301	−0.279	−0.058
+0.341	43	+0.050	−0.067	+0.413	−0.184	−0.118	+0.083	−0.234
+0.458	44	−0.118	+0.240	+0.295	+0.136	−0.198	−0.151	−0.257
+0.337	45	+0.315	+0.338	+0.180	−0.150	−0.239	+0.130	+0.154
+0.389	46	+0.321	+0.246	+0.159	+0.084	−0.110	−0.096	−0.103
+0.333	47	+0.319	+0.558	+0.126	+0.159	+0.130	−0.095	−0.124
+0.367	48	+0.169	+0.135	+0.203	−0.171	−0.143	−0.272	−0.201
+0.450	49	+0.073	−0.329	+0.251	−0.166	−0.222	−0.217	+0.272
+0.252	50	+0.524	+0.105	+0.167	−0.183	+0.165	+0.222	−0.134
+0.384	51	+0.324	−0.189	−0.113	−0.246	+0.327	+0.141	+0.257
+0.348	52	+0.265	+0.291	−0.161	−0.422	−0.094	−0.088	−0.152
+0.425	53	−0.051	−0.167	+0.206	−0.201	+0.143	−0.212	+0.313
+0.254	54	−0.470	+0.218	+0.194	−0.303	−0.219	−0.176	+0.333
+0.378	55	−0.181	−0.229	+0.092	+0.115	−0.228	+0.392	+0.296
+0.272	56	+0.266	−0.243	−0.098	+0.101	−0.082	+0.278	+0.215
+0.330	57	+0.192	−0.230	+0.118	−0.148	+0.414	+0.140	+0.277
+0.247	58	−0.119	+0.258	+0.150	−0.094	+0.590	+0.117	−0.223
+0.534N	59	−0.186	+0.239	−0.161	−0.239	−0.095	+0.089	−0.140
PC of V		14.97	09.67	04.81	05.16	04.94	03.95	03.85

APPENDIX F *(continued)*

CENTROID FACTORS—cont.

	8	9	10	11	12	13	14	15
31	+0.109	−0.182	−0.037	−0.064	−0.206	+0.087	+0.038	−0.112
32	−0.151	+0.235	+0.066	+0.104	+0.235	−0.062	+0.049	+0.118
33	−0.170	−0.053	+0.164	+0.069	−0.175	+0.248	+0.115	+0.089
34	−0.086	+0.066	+0.123	+0.095	−0.067	−0.102	+0.063	−0.160
35	−0.052	−0.081	+0.115	+0.111	−0.057	+0.161	+0.079	+0.177
36	−0.119	−0.076	−0.127	+0.126	−0.118	+0.142	+0.105	−0.196
37	−0.087	+0.058	+0.072	+0.075	−0.132	+0.123	−0.150	−0.256
38	−0.095	+0.071	+0.909	+0.192	−0.069	−0.078	+0.160	+0.067
39	−0.108	+0.192	+0.197	−0.110	+0.086	+0.078	+0.128	+0.209
40	+0.097	+0.207	+0.164	−0.153	+0.146	+0.258	−0.140	−0.190
41	−0.122	+0.102	+0.185	+0.144	−0.122	−0.055	−0.155	−0.201
42	−0.114	+0.126	−0.250	−0.138	−0.151	+0.074	+0.048	+0.147
43	+0.153	+0.289	−0.390	+0.153	−0.214	+0.154	+0.124	−0.077
44	−0.138	+0.137	+0.301	−0.137	+0.128	+0.159	−0.178	+0.129
45	+0.270	+0.361	−0.065	−0.180	−0.141	+0.135	+0.070	+0.120
46	+0.287	−0.249	−0.086	+0.189	+0.181	+0.141	+0.156	+0.344
47	−0.154	−0.206	−0.067	−0.094	−0.216	+0.155	−0.095	+0.110
48	−0.202	+0.201	−0.220	−0.176	−0.106	+0.277	−0.317	−0.177
49	+0.159	−0.162	−0.137	+0.126	+0.193	+0.178	−0.063	+0.125
50	−0.130	−0.148	−0.250	−0.213	−0.119	−0.259	−0.157	+0.233
51	−0.169	−0.067	−0.332	−0.119	−0.149	−0.080	−0.125	−0.085
52	−0.209	+0.255	−0.292	+0.143	−0.138	−0.057	−0.118	+0.055
53	+0.270	+0.165	−0.172	+0.298	+0.072	−0.164	−0.206	+0.072
54	+0.160	−0.154	+0.103	+0.179	−0.161	+0.136	−0.128	+0.072
55	−0.157	+0.189	+0.089	+0.076	−0.080	+0.159	−0.313	+0.133
56	−0.147	−0.250	−0.127	+0.339	−0.340	+0.186	−0.251	+0.139
57	−0.264	−0.288	+0.119	+0.151	+0.057	+0.103	−0.225	+0.149
58	−0.099	+0.346	−0.116	+0.202	+0.058	+0.088	+0.050	−0.182
59	+0.199	−0.298	−0.137	+0.146	−0.205	+0.140	+0.094	−0.125
PC of V	03.34	03.42	03.18	02.60	02.50	02.62	02.17	02.22

Index

afterlife, belief in, 31, 33, 35, 51
agriculture, 24, 29-30
anxiety, and ritual, 35
Apollonianism, 31-36
  influence of, 54-55, 58-64
  and moral order, 50-53
  and technology, 36, 52-53
Asch, S., 42

Benedict, R., 9, 32
Bennett, John W., 1 n.
Bernard, Claude, 63

capital, 63
Carr, E. H., 10
caste, 27-29
  and technology, 37-38
causal analysis, 71-78
  (see also factor analysis;
    system analysis)
causal priority, 67-78
Childe, V. G., 10, 24-26
class, hereditary (see caste)
cluster analysis, 72 n.
Coleman, James, 1 n.
Comte, A., 11
Cornford, F. M., 32 n.
cross-cultural research, 13, 16, 17-19
cultural relativism, 12
cultures
  factor analysis of, 13-19
  functional analysis of, 2-13
  (see also cross-cultural research;
    social systems)

Dickman, Kern, 1 n.
Dionysianism, 32-34, 39
Durkheim, Emile, 2, 6, 11, 52

Evans-Pritchard, E. E., 10 n.

factor analysis, 13-19, 20, 72, 74-75
  (see also causal analysis)
family, historical emphasis on, 10
  (see also lineality; sex dominance)
father right (see lineality)
Fisher, R., 73 n.
Fruchter, B., 72 n.
functional analysis, 2-3, 7-19, 65

Gerth, Hans, 6 n.
Ginsberg, M., 13, 29, 30 n.
Goldschmidt, Walter, 1 n., 10
Gouldner, Alvin W., 8 n., 68, 70, 73, 77
grain cultivation, 24
  (see also agriculture)
Gross, L., 8 n.
group, self and, 43, 45-47

Hamblin, Robert, 1 n.
Harman, H. H., 72 n.
Harsanyi, John C., 61, 68-69, 70, 77
Hobhouse, L. T., 13, 29, 30
Holzinger, K. J., 72 n.
Homans, G. C., 35
Human Relations Area Files, 1, 17, 19
husband rights (see sex dominance)

impulse control, 34, 38, 51-53
  (see also Apollonianism)
individual (see self)

Kaiser, Henry F., 55
Kaplan, Irving, 1 n.
kinship, anthropological research in,
  10, 64
  (see also lineality; sex dominance)
Kroeber, A. L., 9